Winslow

The Mysterious Mesa Murders

Verne Nobles, Sr.

William A. Blum

Acknowledgment

To this day, I am yet to meet a creative person, whether musician, artist, poet or writer, who has brought into their lives that one special person whom, at times, may have criticized or praised their work with complete acceptance of either. I am grateful that I am one of the few who have encountered such a treasure. She is my wife, my editor, my life…Nedene Tucci Nobles.

Verne Nobles, Sr.

Acknowledgment

There have been several mentors who facilitated my career as a writer, but only one I truly respect and rely on, as I continue to grow as a writer. My associate and mentor has, to this day, guided my path as someone who can now call himself a writer. Someone whom avid readers will look for and consider as their author of choice. Thank you Verne Nobles.

William A. Blum

Author's Dedication

To my three sons Vernon, Anthony and Sean. As a father, they each have been my continued inspiration, as well as my greatest challenge, to say the least.

Verne Nobles, Sr.

Author's Dedication

In a very short lifetime, there are few people who enter the path you have chosen to walk. No one can be considered more profound than my wife, Bengie, who has supported all my efforts in choice of career, lifestyle and personal goals. Her warmth and generosity has surpassed all expectations as a life partner. I am truly grateful I encountered this woman in the twilight of my life. Her heartfelt compassion for living has brought me joy and inspiration and become my very soul. I look forward to the continued memories we will share together.

William A. Blum

About the Authors

In 1979, Verne Nobles Sr. was invited to leave his commercial production company in Detroit, Michigan, after producing and directing over 3200 national and international commercials, and join 20th Century Fox. Within two years, Verne had written, produced, and directed three prestigious, wide-screen documentaries for the studio, featuring narration by Orson Welles, Lowell Thomas, and Charlton Heston, with guest appearances by Alex Haley, President Gerald Ford, Louis L'Amour, Dick Van Dyke, Gregory Peck and Margaret Truman, as well as other historical figures. These films were followed by co-producing the television production of Louis L'Amour's "The Shadow Riders" and L'Amour's "Shaughnessy", which would be the stepping stone of a long 65-year journey in the various aspects of the entertainment industry.

About the Authors

William A Blum… There were times when I would sit up in my tower crane two hundred feet in the air, like an eagle and gaze over the landscape. I fixed my eyes at the people below me and wondered what life they had intended for themselves. Construction is one of the most challenging careers with respect to a physical attribute. When I entered this field, I was very young, filled with aspirations and desires to become something more than just a person who operated heavy equipment. I've had several successful businesses and enjoyed the fruits of my labor. During that time, I enjoyed a variety of encounters, but the most difficult of all the tasks I placed before me was sitting down with a pen and paper, creating something people would actually read and find enjoyable.

Author's Photograph by Richard Kelly

Our personal thank you to designer Derry Frost for bringing the Black Darkness evil to the back cover.

Table of Contents

Introduction

Step into the enigmatic world of "WINSLOW: The Mysterious Mesa Murders," where the echoes of the 1947 military DC4 crash resonate through time, intertwining with the present-day murder investigations led by Hopi tribe Ranger Jacin Yazzie. A tale shrouded in mystery and pulsating with the supernatural. The journey unfolds against the stark beauty of Arizona's landscapes, concealing secrets that transcend generations.

In the aftermath of the DC4 crash carrying gold bars and Government scientists, bodies burned beyond recognition, and a cover-up labelling it as pilot error or the wrath of inclement weather, the truth remains buried. Eighty years later, the repercussions of that fateful day resurface in the Hopi Village at Mesa Two, as bodies with inexplicable wounds ignite a chain of events that defy explanation.

Jacin Yazzie, a dedicated Hopi tribe Ranger, finds himself at the forefront of an investigation that leads him down a rabbit hole of conspiracies, hidden agendas, and a possible Columbian connection. As Lieutenant Robb Parker Winslow PD and pathologist Dr. Phillip Torrey join forces, the lines between reality, the unknown blur, and the Navajo Nation become the stage for a high-stakes showdown.

This isn't merely a murder mystery; it's a journey into uncharted territories of ancient cultures, government secrets, and the eerie possibility that beings not of this world may walk among us. The narrative promises to enthral with its rich cultural tapestry, weaving together historical events, speculative fiction, and the deep-rooted heritage of the Navajo and Hopi people.

As you delve into the pages of "WINSLOW," be prepared for a riveting exploration where time is a fluid concept, and the unseen forces guiding the destinies of its characters leave you questioning the boundaries between reality and imagination. The Mysterious Mesa Murders await, calling you into a world where the past casts a long shadow over the present, and the truth is a journey of discovery into the heart of the unknown.

Chapter 1: Prologue - August 13, 1947

The night hangs heavy over the Arizona desert as the USAAF Douglas C-54B Skymaster wrestles with the unforgiving elements. Lightning arcs across the inky sky, illuminating the tumultuous clouds that cling to the heavens. The deafening roar of thunder echoes through the cockpit as the pilot, Captain Jonathan Hastings, fights to maintain control.

Inside the aircraft, the atmosphere is thick with tension. The metallic taste of fear lingers as the plane bucks and shudders in the grip of the storm. The steady hum of engines battles against the violent howl of the wind, creating a dissonant symphony of chaos. Hastings grips the yoke with white-knuckled determination, his eyes squinting through the deluge outside.

Co-pilot Lieutenant Maggi Sullivan scans the instruments with unwavering focus, her gloved hands dancing across switches and levers. Rain batters against the windows, blurring the line between the interior and the tempest beyond. The gravity of their cargo, thirty million in gold bars and bagged coins, hangs in the air—a tangible weight matched only by the perilous circumstances surrounding them.

"Captain, we're losing altitude! We need to climb!" shouts Lieutenant Sullivan over the cacophony of the storm.

Hastings wrestles with the controls, muscles straining against the relentless forces conspiring to bring them down. Lightning cracks across the sky, casting fleeting shadows in the cockpit. The altimeter needle dips perilously, and beads of sweat form on Hastings' forehead.

"Damn it, we can't go higher! We're on the edge of stalling now!" he barks in response.

The Skymaster convulses as if in response to the pilot's words, caught in the grip of an unseen adversary. The turbulence intensifies, and panic tightens its grip on the crew. The radio crackles with the anxious voices of the crew members—faint whispers against the roaring tempest.

Suddenly, a blinding flash of lightning reveals an ominous silhouette in the distance. Another aircraft, a spectre in the storm, materializes out of the darkness. The seconds stretch into an eternity as the two vessels hurtle toward an inevitable collision.

The second vessel drops below the DC4, but not before the sudden impact under the ill-fated military plane now being pushed upward when it comes, creating a deafening sound of metal on metal. The Skymaster and the mysterious intruder become a maelstrom of chaos, their fate sealed in the heart of the storm.

The night air shrieks with the fury of a relentless storm over the vast Arizona desert. The fiery wreckage of the military DC4, now a partly twisted metal monument to tragedy, lies a wing partly torn away from the fuselage, fuel feeding the fire, and engine parts scattered across the rugged landscape of the Navajo Reservation. In the aftermath of the crash, the secrets held within the charred, remaining fuselage unfold like a dark omen.

The passengers' bodies, once full of life and purpose, now lie at the edge of death, portals.

Amid the carnage, the passengers' identities remain shrouded in mystery, their existence reduced to whispers carried away by the wind. The eventual official narrative, a hasty label of pilot error or the wrath of inclement weather, only deepens the enigma surrounding that fateful night.

Among the debris, the gold bars glint, remnants of a cargo that never reached its intended destination. The thirty million dollars in precious metal, now a symbol of lost fortune, whispers tales of a conspiracy that transcends the boundaries of the crash itself. The wreckage tells a story of a secret government cover-up, a tale buried in the desolation of the Arizona desert.

As the dawn threatens to break, casting a pale glow over the wreckage, the scene remains frozen in time. It is a tableau of destruction, where the echoes of the storm still linger, the ghosts of the passengers and their unfulfilled destinies haunting the barren land.

Two military officers, silent sentinels of the crash site, stand amidst the wreckage, their yellow rain slickers over their uniforms battered by the storm. Their duty is to safeguard the remnants of the military DC4, but their expressions betray a sense of unease. The weight of the unknown presses upon them as if the crash had opened the door to a world unseen.

A division of the Military Seabees has arrived before daybreak, and a dozen or so large trucks surround the crash site. A number of jeeps have also arrived with both military and government inspectors. Some MP units have set up a perimeter around the site. While the Seabee team had come with a D7 cat bulldozer, a Hough HA loader, a 1946 international harvester KB6 tractor with low-bed trailers loaded with an Allis Chalmers C model loader, and a Hough HA loader, a D7 Caterpillar, which will bulldoze and bury any parts left behind. The crew works around the Military inspectors; the plan is to have the crash field cleaned and everything loaded and on the road before nightfall.

The two military officers, Major Jon Kwahu and Colonel Robert Harris, along with half a dozen federal agents, had arrived at the site as daylight searched for a new day.

As Major Jon Kwahu visually explores the site, his gaze fixes upon the twisted metal and scattered debris, witnessing the aftermath of a tragedy that defies explanation. The government investigation team, summoned to assess the wreckage, moves efficiently, cataloging the remnants and recovering what they deem necessary for further scrutiny.

The wreckage, though a somber testament to the storm's wrath, holds the residue of a covert operation. The government agents comb through the scene, their faces hidden behind stoic masks. They salvage what they can, leaving only fragments behind, and erase any visible trace of their clandestine involvement.

As the investigation unfolds, Jon and his fellow officer exchange glances, silently acknowledging the enigma that surrounds the crash. The truth seems elusive, slipping through their fingers like the sand that will eventually bury the remnants of the military DC4. Little do they know, the events of that morning will become a lingering mystery, casting shadows that stretch far beyond the desolation of the Arizona desert.

Major Kwahu is not a stranger to the desert; he grew up in villages scattered throughout the four main Mesas. They are in the process, along with several photographers, of surveying the scene with furrowed brows. The wind whispers through the twisted metal, carrying with it the echoes of the deceased. Major Kwahu's eyes, filled with a mix of sorrow and curiosity, trace the contours of the destroyed aircraft, searching for answers in the chaos. Unspoken words linger in the air as they exchange glances, each aware of the uncharted territory they are about to traverse.

Their investigation is meticulous, capturing every detail that remains at the crash site. Photographs are taken, measurements are recorded, and artefacts are carefully collected. The military intelligence team, led by Major Kwahu, tries to understand the gravity of the situation. The wreckage tells a story of tragedy but also hints at something more profound—an enigma that demands unraveling.

As the investigation progresses, Major Kwahu's Hopi heritage connects him to the land in ways others might not comprehend. The whispers of the desert seem to speak to him, urging him to delve deeper into the mysteries that surround the crash. His upbringing within the Hopi villages grants him insight into the cultural nuances of the area, and he intuits that the answers they seek might be intertwined with the ancient secrets held by the land.

Colonel Harris, a seasoned military officer, observes the proceedings with a stoic demeanor. His focus is on the official aspects of the investigation, but he can't dismiss the palpable sense of unease that permeates the air. The wind, carrying tales of the past, whispers of a conspiracy that reaches beyond the stormy night of the crash.

Little do Major Kwahu and Colonel Harris know that the events unfolding in the Arizona desert will cast a long shadow over the years to come, becoming a mystery that transcends the boundaries of time and space.

The sky overhead begins to lighten, revealing the scorched earth and the remnants of lives extinguished. The air hums with a strange energy as if the very atmosphere holds the secrets of that night. The crash site, now a stage for unfolding mysteries, awaits the revelation of truths that will eventually transcend time.

Amid the wreckage, a small metallic object catches the Major's attention. He bends down to retrieve it, revealing a military insignia tarnished by the fire. The symbol hints at a deeper connection, a thread linking the tragedy to a complex web of military secrets.

The Major examines the insignia, and a voice echoes from the shadows. It is a young tribal leader, Hopi Elder Kaya Nahimana, who has been drawn to the crash site by an inexplicable force. Kaya Nahimana's presence adds another layer to the unfolding enigma, as if the ancient spirits of the land have guided him to the heart of the mystery.

"Strange things happen in these parts," Kaya Nahimana speaks with calm certainty, his eyes scanning the wreckage as if deciphering an ancient tablet. "This crash is more than it seems. There are whispers in the wind, Major. Whispers that speak of a truth to be hidden in the folds of time."

The Major, speaking in the native tongue, tells the young Hopi tribesman, "I feel it also, my brother." Colonel Reynolds looks at the Major, skepticism etched on his face but a flicker of curiosity in his eyes. He turns, looking to ask the young Hopi.

"How did you get past the MPs? This is a restricted area."

The young tribesman looks down at the Colonel's boots and answers in a soft voice.

"The land you stand on is Hopi Land; the question is, what right do all of you have to restrict my boots from my land?"

The Major, in his native tongue, talks to the young tribesman, and he walks away with an MP by his side. The collision of the Colonel's and Major's perspectives, science against spirituality, sets the stage for a complex investigation that will unravel not only the events of the crash but also, in the far future, the very fabric of unexplored reality.

The mystery of the crash has just begun its descent into the depths of the unknown, where the past and present intertwine in a dance of shadows and revelations. The desert, a silent witness to the unfolding drama, will hold its secrets close for over 78 years, waiting for those who understand the desert to unravel the threads of fate.

The relentless Arizona sun, now fully ascendant, casts an unyielding glow over the military DC4's wreckage. The twisted metal skeleton, marred by the violence of the crash and the subsequent inferno, stands as a haunting testament to the mysterious events that will unfold over time.

The two military officers continue their meticulous examination of the wreckage. The Colonel, driven by a logical mind, seeks answers amongst the tangible evidence scattered across the desert floor. The Major, guided by a deeper connection to his Hopi heritage, feels the presence of unseen forces lingering in the air.

The tattered logbook discovered within the remains of the fuselage becomes a focal point of their investigation. The Colonel carefully pores over its pages, uncovering cryptic notations and irregularities in the flight details. The cargo manifest hints at a covert operation, raising questions about the true nature and actual destination of the doomed mission. He carefully places the logbook in a plastic evidence bag.

"There are questions about this mission that continue to leave me to wonder what exactly these civilian passengers were doing on a military cargo plane. Hopefully, the answers are locked in these scorched pages, and somehow, we need to decipher it."

The Major takes the bag from the Colonel and places it in a leather case he has shouldered to collect items found in the dust as he continues along the path of scorched seats, responding to the Colonel's assumption.

"This crash disturbed more than the metal and sand; it disrupted the spirits that watch over this land." The Colonel responds sarcastically, with fewer mystic assumptions.

"Whatever!"

The Major, now standing in the aft compart and looking back up the row of scorched seats,

"One thing that does not make any sense at this point is how the bodies here in the fuselage were turned to dust, separate from the crew in the cockpit, whose bodies were burned but not to dust."

It is thought to have been a separate event after the flames had dissipated within the cabin. As the Colonel continues to look about the pilot's cabin area, Major Kwahu, mostly to hear his words out loud, shares his observations.

"If this plane was involved in a mid-air collision with another aircraft, then where did this other ship go down? At this point, there are no other reports of another crash within a 60-mile radius. With no clear landing path for the pilot to bring this damaged ninety-three foot ten inch, thirty-nine thousand pound ship in on its belly?"

"How did it virtually end up falling out of the sky perfectly horizontal to this very site." "That is impossible, but here we are."

"Apparently, the raging storm had eventually put the crash flames out." The colonel forward turns, asking,

"What was that, Major?"

"Nothing, sir, just thinking out loud."

Their conversation is interrupted by a distant murmur from the approaching group of villagers. Hopi people from a nearby village, drawn by an invisible thread, begin to gather at the guarded, protected edge of the crash site. Among them is Kaya, an elder known for her wisdom and connection to the ancient prophecies. The bizarre contrast of modern construction equipment with a crane reaching the dark clouds stands between the Hopi tribal members and the ill-fated DC 4.

The two officers exit the ship and exchange wary glances as the Hopi gather, sensing an unspoken understanding that the events unfolding are not confined to the realm of human comprehension. The air seems charged with an otherworldly tension as if the crash had torn a rift between the seen and the unseen.

As the Hopi members assemble, the Major asks the Colonel to let him handle the villagers. He sends an MP to bring their leader closer. As a woman is escorted to the wreckage, their eyes meet. Jon sees a depth of knowledge and an acknowledgment of a reality beyond the grasp of military protocol and logical deductions. Within the Hopi People, the crash seems to set in motion a series of events that transcend the boundaries of human perception… Why?

The woman looks at the young Hopi officer and asks, "As a boy, were you taught the ways of the spirits who guide our people?"

Major Kwahu looks into the woman's eyes and speaks softly, "I was."

The woman bends down and picks up a handful of hot sand. "This crushed thing out there that has fallen to Mother Earth has awakened the wickedness and evil of the black darkness from the third world. In another time, our people escaped this wickedness and emerged up into the fourth world for the promise of this land. Masauwu was the master of the fourth world and was there to give our people stewardship over the land. He was known to the Hopi as Skeleton Man, the spirit of death, the keeper of fire, and the guardian of the door to the fifth world. Masauwu is a deity to be feared but respected. At that time, we were given the path to this world. That is when Tawa, the Sun Spirit, the Creator who formed the first world out of Tokpella, the endless space and all its original inhabitants of the universe, came to drive the darkness back from emerging into the fourth world, sealing its wickedness in the third world. I am here to tell you what you already know. Once again, it now spreads across the land of the Hopi and must be returned to the depths from where it has been released. It will eventually bring its wickedness and deadly wars to consume all life as we know it. It will not stop until it has infected the minds of everything living."

She lets the sand fall from her fingers and continues, "On this land, at this place, at this time, a great evil has come from beyond the heavens. The spirits will not sleep until this evil is banished and a great Hopi warrior has come to face the black darkness and send it back to the depth from where it has risen".

She looks up at the Major, touches his chest with her finger, and speaks quietly, "Below this uniform beats a Hopi heart that hears the whispers in the wind and knows that what I speak is not a myth but the truth."

She turns and walks back to the Hopi people who have gathered and now embraced her.

The presence of the Hopi woman's words adds a layer of complexity to the unfolding mystery. The collision of military secrecy and ancient spirituality creates a tapestry of intrigue that demands unraveling. This crash is not merely an isolated incident but the epicenter of a convergence between worlds—a collision of timelines and realities that tests the resolve of those seeking the truth. The Colonel, somewhat curious about what the woman had said to the young Major, looks on.

The Major glances at the Hopi, who are now slowly moving away from the guarded area, before answering. "Something happened here in the night, far beyond the crash that took the lives of passengers and crew. We may never know what actually happened in the storm, but what took place here after the crash has mysteriously affected the tribal beliefs."

The Colonel's interest and attention are drawn to the sounds as the last of the ill-fated plane is readied to be loaded.

Night threatens the late afternoon sky, and the majority of the inspection crews have pulled out. Major Kwahu watches as the remains of the once mighty USAAF Douglas C-54B Skymaster are prepared to be packed and transported for storage in some warhorses in another desert. Its mission untold its secrets, searching in the desert's winds for the truth.

An American 275 BC crane pulls on the site, the two officers watch as it lifts the Pratt & Whitney engine, along with the wings and fuselage, onto a flatbed now that the inspection has been completed. The Seabee crew has completed their job, packed up, and the parade of equipment heads into the night. The tale of the DC4 crash, the missing gold, and the lives lost will echo through the decades. Only the towering Mesas hold any sign of the unfortunate crash.

The desert, with its secrets buried in the sands, holds its breath as if anticipating the next chapter in a story that spans decades and dimensions. The year is now 2025. The journey into the heart of the Mesa Murders is about to begin, and the unraveling mystery promises to reveal truths that defy explanation 78 years earlier.

Chapter 2: Murder One

In the Toba Arizona State Bank, the atmosphere is thick with the weight of transactions and the buzz of daily activities. A small, wooden date holder with a white insert card reads "August 11, 2025." A man's hand enters, placing a personal bank check on the counter in front of the date box. He turns it over and signs the back of it, then clips several business-type checks to a separate deposit slip.

A tall man with sculptured Roman features, dark skin, and an overwhelmingly muscular Navajo body steps away from the high counter. With a check and deposit slip in his hand he walks to the line where several women are waiting their turn at the teller windows. The younger woman in front of him smiles at the man before moving closer to the window and approaching the teller. She hands over a deposit slip and cash. The teller processes the deposit through the register machine and gives the woman a receipt. Smiling again at the man, she exits.

As the man steps up to the counter, the teller says something from behind the Plexiglas window. He places the check and deposit slips with the other checks through the small opening.

"Good morning, Margret. I'd like to make these deposits and cash a personal check for one hundred dollars, ten and twenties," Jacin says.

He glances at the young man who is standing behind an older gentleman at the next window, about to complete his transaction. As the teller nods and smiles at the gentleman, he turns and walks away. Margret places the deposit slip in the drawer and, before cashing the check, turns to the other teller. The young man moves up to the window as the teller turns away and shows Margret a document.

As the two tellers talk, the young man reaches into his pocket and takes out a piece of paper. Jacin catches a glimpse of the revolver stuck in the young man's pants. It's obvious the young man is a little nervous.

"Is this your first bank robbery?" Jacin asks quietly.

"What?" the young man responds, startled.

Margret signs the sheet attached to the document.

"Your first bank robbery? If you hand the teller that note, you've committed a federal crime, and it'll be worse because you have a weapon," Jacin advises.

The teller places the document in the drawer and turns to face the young man as Margret cashes Jacin's check.

"Can I help you, sir?" the teller asks the young man.

The young man looks around, backs away from the window, and heads for the exit door. Jacin takes the cash from Margret and turns to watch the young man. An older man grabs the young man by the arm as he reaches the door.

"Where's the money?" the older man demands.

"I can't do it," the young man replies.

"Damn you, kid!" The older man pushes him aside, pulls out a gun, and points it at the guard, who has been looking out the window and has now turned to see what's happening.

"This is a holdup!" the older man shouts.

The guard reaches for his gun, and just as the older man is about to fire, the young man pushes him away. The shot hits the guard in the leg, and he falls back.

Jacin, who has drawn his gun from under his coat, commands, "Drop the gun!"

The older man, still brandishing the weapon, confronts Jacin. The young man grabs the older man's arm for the second time as he fires. The bullet hits the safe glass behind Jacin. Instinctively, Jacin fires his weapon, preventing the man from shooting again. The older man falls backward, holding his stomach. Through the double bank doors, Jacin sees a car speeding away from the curb.

"Throw your gun on the floor, take your belt off, and wrap it around the guard's leg... NOW!" Jacin orders the young man.

The young man takes out his gun and drops it. Jacin moves to the older man and picks up his gun. Jacin yells, "Call an ambulance!"

The young man moves to the guard and wraps the belt around the guard's leg, and together they tighten it. Jacin picks up the young man's gun and sets both on the high counter.

A police siren can be heard as a patrol car pulls up, stopping in front of the bank.

***

The next morning, Jacin Yazzie, the Hopi tribe Ranger who was involved in the bank shooting, emerges from the quietude of his Hopi reservation home bordering the city of Winslow.

Living with his wife Kele, son Mato, and their Australian Shepherd dog named 'Dog,' Jacin's home is a typical Hopi stucco one-story structure with two bedrooms, a dining room, a living room, a kitchen, and a barn. As the morning light filters through the desert landscape, Jacin, dressed in his Hopi ranger uniform, goes about his routine.

"Good morning, Winslow. This is your morning wake-up call. I'm Hayward Dean, and this is your Friday report," the radio personality announces.

Next to the radio, the coffee pot's red light blinks. Jacin grabs the pot and pours a cup of coffee into his favorite mug, a chipped white ceramic cup with a faded Hopi ranger symbol.

Jacin walks quietly through the house. He stops at the doorway of the dark bedroom and looks in at his wife, Kele, who is still asleep. Her peaceful form is wrapped under a white sheet, and the morning light just begins to touch her serene face, highlighting her delicate Navajo features. Her long, black hair fans out on the pillow, contrasting with the pale linen.

He enters the room and kneels beside her, his rugged face softening as he watches her sleep. He gently brushes a strand of hair from her forehead. She stirs slightly, a small smile forming, but she doesn't wake. Satisfied that she is resting peacefully, he turns and walks back to the kitchen, listening to the radio and absorbing the news broadcast.

"A family of four was located yesterday after they had been missing for five days. A flash flood caught their pickup and carried it away for several miles from US40. Their seven-year-old son said it was the best adventure ever. I'm sure Mom and Dad did not feel the same."

Jacin Yazzie stands at the window, looking out at the morning sky, which hints at a rainstorm in the distance. He wears the uniform of the Navajo Nation Police, with a patch on his shoulder and a brass badge on his chest. He picks up a brown hand-painted bowl from the sideboard, takes out a biscuit, and then turns his attention to the dark bedroom off the kitchen. He sips his coffee and bites into the biscuit.

"Bad news for Northern Arizona is the weather is about to add to your cost of business," the radio host continues. "Real estate property owners fear that mandatory flood insurance premiums will slow down their market and diminish property values. Flood insurance costs continue to disqualify some potential buyers."

Jacin's gaze shifts to the horizon as he listens. The radio host's voice turns somber, warning about impending storms and urging residents to prepare.

Jacin takes another sip of coffee, absorbing the weight of the news. Then the broadcast shifts again, this time with urgency.

"Hold on... Just in... Early this morning, prisoners Richard Moran and Jake Miller killed a guard and escaped from Winslow's top security prison. As we get more on this, we will keep you informed."

The tension in the air thickens. Jacin takes a last bite of his biscuit and listens to the news report.

"An unrelated story out of Tuba City. A robbery attempt ended in a shooting at the Arizona State Bank yesterday," the radio voice announces.

Jacin walks to the door of the dark bedroom and looks in again as he listens.

"Fortunately, a Ranger from the Hopi Reservation was in the bank and wounded the would-be thief," the radio host continues.

"It's believed that another man escaped in a blue Jeep Wrangler. The Ranger gave credit to a young man who fought the bank robber and saved the life of the bank guard."

He walks back to the kitchen, opens the refrigerator, and takes out a packet of dog food. The refrigerator door is adorned with pictures of Kele and Jacin embracing and another with a young boy. With the dog food in a bowl, he picks up his coffee and steps outside. The family dog, an Australian Shepherd, sits near the door, waiting patiently for breakfast.

As Jacin bends over to put the food down, a large, long shadow approaches. He looks up to see a tall figure on a Mustang horse. It's Ranger Paco Nez, Jacin's best friend and part-time Deputy. Paco, tall, muscular, and ruggedly handsome, slides off the horse and greets Jacin with a nod.

"Is that fresh coffee I smell?" Paco asks, his eyes gleaming with familiarity and history.

"Just brewed," Jacin replies with a smile.

Paco cocks his head, listening to the voice on the radio. "On a lighter note. Beverly Wilson is online. She has a school project, and she wants to know how big the Navajo Nation is."

Jacin turns and walks into the house. Paco stands, listening to the radio. His horse tries to nibble the dog food, but the Shepherd growls and pushes its snout away.

"Well, Beverly, the Navajo Nation covers about 17,544,500 acres and spans across Arizona, Southeast Utah, and Northwestern New Mexico. The population of the Hopi Reservation in Arizona is 6,946,685," the radio host explains.

Inside, Jacin continues to get ready and reaches over to turn off the radio.

Paco yells after him, "I was listening to that. I didn't know we had so much land. I thought the white man took it all."

Jacin exits the house, shaking his head. He is carrying a cup of coffee for Paco and holding a jacket. He hands Paco the coffee and walks to his cruiser, placing the jacket and his tablet in the back seat.

"What were you doing back when we were learning about our people in school?" Jacin asks.

Paco grins. "There was this girl and..."

A man's voice squawks from a hand radio in the kitchen, the message unintelligible. Jacin interrupts Paco and walks back into the house.

"If I remember correctly, there was always 'a girl'. I do not know how you made it to graduation," Jacin says with a chuckle.

Paco finishes his coffee and continues talking. He pauses at the door, looking back in, "There was this smart girl, not as beautiful, but smart..."

The hand radio in Jacin's house crackles to life again, a disembodied voice from the dispatcher permeating the air.

"101 dispatch... 101," the voice calls out, urgency in its tone, a prelude to the day's events. Paco's arrival has already interrupted Jacin's morning routine. He answers the call, "Dispatch, this is Jacin. Go ahead."

The dispatcher's voice relays a request for assistance from the Department of Public Safety (DPS) regarding a call on Mesa Two. Jacin's brow furrows as he processes the information. "A tribal elder has reported a disturbing discovery – two bodies on a cliff shelf on the east side of Mesa Two." The desert holds secrets that refuse to remain buried.

Paco, now inside with Jacin, listens to the conversation. His presence is a given; where one goes, the other follows. The dispatcher continues providing details. Jacin nods to Paco, affirming his commitment.

"You working today?" Jacin asks Paco.

Paco, enjoying the coffee, responds, "Well, that depends."

Jacin slips on his holster and gun. "We have a couple of bodies."

Paco takes another sip before answering, "Are they dead?"

"Seems that way. Where?" Jacin heads for the door.

"Mesa Two. A prisoner escaped WSP, and the CPS force are all headed for South Canyon with the FBI and state police. DPS wants us to check out Mesa Two."

Jacin walks to the police cruiser, and Paco follows. "I'm working, but I didn't bring my badge."

Jacin opens the cruiser door. Paco, standing nearby, finishes his coffee. Jacin places the radio in the front compartment and looks at Paco. "Open the door and get in."

Paco gets in as Jacin calls, "Dog, come." The dog jumps in on Paco and then to the back seat. Jacin starts the cruiser. Paco closes the door, and they pull out.

"What about your horse?" Jacin asks.

"He'll walk home. You know my horse has a name," Paco replies.

"Yeah," Jacin acknowledges.

"Why do you call your dog 'Dog'?" Paco asks.

"That's his name... Dog," Jacin explains.

"I'd name him Gah. He is fast, like a rabbit. Gah is a good name," Paco suggests.

"He is a dog, not a rabbit, so his name is Dog," Jacin says firmly.

"Stupid name," Paco mutters under his breath. "From now on, I'm going to call him Gah." He takes a last sip of his coffee and looks for a place to put the cup.

"Department of Public Safety... I think it was a political move to let the Arizona State Police form the DPS to stick their force into tribal affairs," Paco comments, folding his arms.

"They have done a hell of a lot to control the crime all over the Navajo Nation," Jacin counters.

"They think the prisoner's headed for the canyon," Paco says.

"Yes. Someone saw one of them near the River Launch," Jacin confirms.

"Good place to hide if you know what you're doing," Paco notes.

"Do I get a gun today?" Paco asks.

"No badge, no gun," Jacin replies.

Paco looks out at the desert and closes his eyes as the cruiser continues on. Jacin turns onto a narrow road, passing a sign that reads "Hopi Settlement—Mesa Two 45 Miles." The road up the Mesa is narrow, and the valley vista in the morning offers a spectacular view as the coming storm mixes with the desert colors.

Unaware of the unfolding events regarding the prison break reported on the morning news, Jacin approaches Mesa Two with solemn determination. The call of duty guides him, and as he steps onto the sacred ground, the shadows of the past seem to converge with the urgency of the present. The bright morning sun has brought the beauty of the desert out of the night, revealing the ancient mysteries of towering mesas.

The long journey to Mesa Two finds Paco and Dog resting. Jacin awakens Paco as they reach Mesa Two landing. He pulls up to the Ponsi Hall Community Center and stops, looking out where a tribal elder awaits him. Jacin exits the vehicle, reaches into the back seat to get his tablet, opens it, and types something. Paco gets out, leaves the door open, and looks at Dog.

"Come on, Gah," Paco calls.

The dog sits there with a curious look on his face and doesn't move. Jacin yells to Dog, "Dog out." Dog jumps out, landing at Paco's boots.

The threesome walks to the edge of the Mesa and joins the elder, whose wrinkled face could tell many stories about the history of the Hopi people of Arizona. About fifty feet below, on a rocky ledge, are two bodies. The elder, a figure of wisdom weathered by years, stands above the tragic scene. The landscape stretches before them, a tableau of ancient secrets and the weight of unspoken truths.

"Morning, Ranger," the elder greets.

"Charlie," Jacin responds.

"My grandson and I were on a walk talk. When the sun came up, I looked down, and they were there. I sent my grandson to wake up the security guard," the elder explains.

"Did either of you see anyone else?" Jacin asks.

"No one. They just showed up. Seen a lot of spooky stuff here over the years. I told security to close the Community Center. The man is useless. He should try sleeping at home," the elder says.

Jacin smiles at the thought. "Spooky stuff..." He places his hand on the man's shoulder. "You want me to send for someone to pick you up?"

"Walked here the first time when I was nine, and for the last eighty years, these feet have found their way here and home," the elder responds.

"The spirits are restless today, Ranger Yazzie," the elder remarks, his eyes reflecting a mix of concern and knowing.

Jacin nods, acknowledging the symbiotic relationship between the land, the people, and the unseen forces that govern their lives. As he approaches the scene at the edge of the high Mesa, the wind carries whispers of the past, intertwining with the urgency of the present.

The elder turns and starts back towards the village. He pauses. "Get those bodies off our Mesa... Bad for business," he says and continues on.

Paco, who has walked along the edge, joins Jacin and Dog as he looks down at the ledge.

"I suppose you want me to go down there." Jacin hands Paco the tablet. "We'll use the car bumper winch hoist. Get some pictures."

Paco puts on the harness and walks to the edge, the cable trailing behind him. As he reaches the edge, he cautiously steps over. The cable goes taut, and Paco puts pressure on it as he leans back with his feet on the cliff side.

"Do I get hazardous pay for this?" Paco calls up.

Jacin gets in the cruiser and starts the engine. "Only if the cable breaks."

Jacin operates the hand switch, releasing the safety lock and slowly lowering Paco. As Paco descends, he reaches rock shelf and peers into the valley far below.

"Hold it there," Paco instructs as he hangs in the air, examining the bodies on the rocky ledge. Taking out the tablet, he captures a few wide photographs, focusing on the back of each man's head where blood has gathered in small holes.

"I think they were shot in the back of the head," Paco yells up to Jacin.

Paco then zooms in the lens, capturing detailed shots of the bodies and the ground around the two mangled men. The tablet displays the gruesome scene – blood-soaked, torn pant legs and ripped shirt sleeves revealing deep cuts on their arms and chests.

Jacin and Dog stand at the edge of the crater, looking down at Paco and waiting for any additional information.

"Anything else?" Jacin calls down.

Paco, still on the cliff's edge, leans down to get another close-up of the hole at the base of one of the men's heads.

"Yes," Paco yells up. "There are two empty backpacks next to the bodies."

A storm brewing in the distance, Jacin removes a tarp from the cruiser and passes it down to Paco, directing him to cover the bodies with the tarp.

The wind whispers through the sparse vegetation, carrying with it the haunting echoes of an unspoken tragedy. Jacin, his face etched with a mix of determination and concern, waits for his friend's response. Soon after, Paco yells to Jacin to bring him up. "I covered them, and I think we have what we need." Once back on the cliff's edge, he removes the harness and hands Jacin the tablet.

"Murder, no doubt about it." Paco hands Jacin the tablet.

The eerie glow of the sun's filtered, clouded light illuminates the Cliffside as Jacin and Paco meticulously examine the photos.

One particular photo of one of the bodies reveals the intricate details of a few of the wounds visible below at the pant cuffs. Photos of the hole at the back of the neck seem to be a macabre signature that speaks of a methodical hand, possibly a Columbian madman's signature. The wind carries the faint scent of juniper, mingling with the tension that hangs in the air.

Jacin grimaces at the macabre scene pictured in the various photos. His assumption lingers in the air. "Probably drug mules," he finally comments. Paco quickly responds. "They decided to go into business for themselves and got a bullet in the head," Jacin closes the tablet and calls Dog, who has stood guard over the cliff's edge. "Maybe, if we're right, the jurisdiction shifts to the Winslow police department." "Once the bodies are transported to the Morgue in Winslow for further examination, I am sure pathologist Doc Torrey will give us more justified answers." "Let's pack it up; there is nothing else for us here."

As the first droplets of rain begin to fall, Jacin reaches for his radio. "Dispatch, this is Jacin Yazzie. I need to get in touch with Lieutenant Robb Parker from Winslow Police on tack One." The radio crackles to life, and Lieutenant Robb Parker's voice resonates through the speaker. "This is Parker. What's going on, Jacin?"

Jacin, his words measured, replies, "We've got a crime scene here, Robb. Two bodies about 50 feet down on a cliffside with strange, deliberate wounds. I need you and Doctor Torrey to take a look at what I found here at Mesa Two. I've called in the fire rescue crew to retrieve the bodies and get them to Winslow tonight."

Without hesitation, Lieutenant Parker responds, "Are they your people?"

Jason answers, "No."

Parker asks "More border trash?"

Jacin responds, "I'm not sure. Something's bothering me. I need you to take a look."

"I'll see you in the morning at the morgue." Lieutenant Parker adds.

The call from DPS regarding the prison break is a sinister backdrop to the unfolding investigation. The convergence of events, the discovery of bodies, and the prison break paint a complex canvas that hints at a deeper connection. Something in the wind pulls at Jason's thoughts.

Meanwhile, on the outskirts of Winslow, the Department of Public Safety (DPS) and state police mobilize with a shared purpose. The prison break, an unforeseen twist in the narrative, demands a swift response. The escaped prisoners, driven by desperation and the rugged terrain, are believed to have set their course toward the Grand Canyon.

As the DPS and state police surge forward, the pursuit of escaped prisoners becomes a race against time, set against the backdrop of the expansive Arizona landscape. The Grand Canyon looms as both a destination and a potential refuge for the fugitives while the echoes of the prison break reverberate through the arid air.

Chapter 3: Prison Break

The collaborative effort between the Hopi tribal Ranger, Winslow Police, Lieutenant Robb Parker unfolds against the backdrop of the coming storm. The shared determination to unravel the mystery bridges the gap between ancient traditions and modern law enforcement.

The Mesa Two murder, shrouded in darkness and ritualistic wounds, marks the beginning of a journey into the unknown, where the past and present collide in the pursuit of truth.

The underlying relationships between the characters become a guiding force. Together, Jacin, Paco, and Lieutenant Robb Parker have faced the unknown many times in their shared past, propelling them forward into the heart of the mystery that unfolded on the cliffside in the towering desert Mesas.

As the rain continues to cascade over the desert, Jacin and Paco make their way to the ranger station, seeking refuge from the downpour. The atmosphere inside the station is tense as the thunderstorm mixes with the hum of fluorescent lights, casting a stark contrast to the storm outside. Deputy Ranger Karen Masawepimana diligently works at her desk, looking up as Jacin and Paco enter along with Dog. Dog shakes the rain away and heads for his place down the hall by the back door.

She hands Jacin half a dozen messages, and he glances at them. Paco takes off his wet jacket, hangs it on the rack near the door, and walks to a desk to turn on the computer and monitor. Karen asks Jacin, "Did you get the call from DPS dispatch?" Looking closely at the messages, he answers, "Yes, as well as an alert online." Karen picks up another note. "Oh yes, Masichuvio called. The wild dogs are at his chickens again. They somehow got into the coop, and he is angry with a shotgun."

Jacin responds, "Tell Grey Deer I will send someone out there today. Call Makia." He removes his rain-soaked jacket and approaches Karen with a folder and the tablet clutched in his hand. He speaks with a sense of urgency, "Karen, two bodies found on Mesa Two have been taken to the Morgue. It could be just another border killing, but I am not sure. I need you to take a look at what we found up there."

Karen, accustomed to Jacin's no-nonsense demeanor, takes the folder and tablet, her eyes scanning the details of the crime scene photos and report. The peculiar wounds and the intricate nature of the murders pique her interest. "This is... different. What are we dealing with here?" she inquires, "a Columbian ritualistic murder gang to handle the runaway mules?"

Jacin, rainwater dripping from his uniform, explains, "I'm not entirely sure. The wounds are unusual, and it feels like there's a connection to something bigger. We need to do some cartel gang research." As the room settles into an uneasy calm, Jacin and

Karen exchange a glance that speaks volumes. The mysteries of Mesa Two and the chaos of the prison break are now intricately entwined, and the unraveling threads threaten to lead them into an even darker abyss.

As Karen delves into the files, a radio on her desk crackles to life with updates about the prison break. The news adds another layer of complexity to the unfolding events. Escaped prisoners from Winslow are on the loose, their desperate flight further complicating the investigation into the Mesa Two murders.

Jacin starts down the hall as Paco gets up and moves to sit down across from Karen, who is looking over Jacin's tablet. Paco comments, "I went down the side of the Mesa on a cable and took the photos." She looks up at Paco. "You're dripping on my desk."

Jacin yells from his office, "Paco, check with the morgue and see if the bodies have arrived." "Karen, come into my office and see if we can make some sense out of this killing. Columbia gangs to chase down runaways or something else."

Deputy Ranger Karen enters Jacin's office and takes a seat at the roundtable. Her gaze shifts from the murder files to Jacin, and she remarks, "This is turning into one hell of a day."

Paco looks up from his desk and offers his opinion. "Are you sure the prison break and the killing aren't connected?"

Jacin, the weight of the mysteries pressing on his shoulders, replies, "I can't say for certain, but it's too coincidental. We need to keep an eye on both of these situations. The storm outside might be the least of our worries." As the rain intensifies outside the ranger station, Jacin and Karen huddle over the files while Paco researches Colombian gang cults on his computer.

The tension inside the ranger station escalates as Jacin and Karen delve deeper into the peculiar murder files and recent Colombian gang activities. The radio continues its sporadic updates on the prison break, casting a shadow of unrest over the room. Unbeknownst to them, the storm outside is not the only tempest brewing. Again, we can hear Dog growling and then continuing to bark at the back door.

As Paco approaches Jacin's office, two shots blast through, shattering the relative calm of the parking lot outside. Jacin immediately reacts, urging Karen to take cover. He grabs his Beretta and heads for the rear office door. "Get a rifle or stay down," he commands, his voice steady with authority.

As Jacin cautiously approaches the back door, the night air is shattered by the crack of a pistol, followed by the booming blast of a shotgun. His faithful companion Dog stands by his side, growling low in warning. With a quick tug, Jacin pushes the door ajar, enough to peer out into the rain-drenched parking lot. The heavy downpour has transformed the once-solid pavement into a treacherous sea of mud.

Before him lies a scene of chaos and danger. Ranger Ahote, a Hopi police officer, sprawls in the muck, clearly injured. The windshield and driver's side window of the police cruiser are shattered by the force of the shot. Across the lot, a second cruiser sits with its trunk yawning open.

Jacin's gaze locks onto a tall, burly figure emerging from the rain—a man with a shock of blond hair and beard clad in a sodden prison shirt. Gripped tightly in his hands is a shotgun, and he is closing in on the fallen ranger, who struggles to rise. The man scoops up the ranger's Glock from the mud with casual menace, pointing the shotgun at the young officer.

In a heartbeat, Jacin springs into action. The door swings wide as he unleashes a shot that narrowly misses the man's head but shatters one of the rooftop lights on the cruiser, scattering glass and drawing blood. In retaliation, the man fires back, blowing a gaping hole through the station door, sending debris flying and plunging the area into chaos.

Seconds later, Jacin emerges from cover, his weapon drawn and ready, just as the assailant bolts for the ranger's SUV, engine growling. With mud and rocks spewing from spinning wheels, the vehicle lurches backward towards the road. Jacin aims once more, each shot ringing out like thunder as he splinters the SUV's front and rear windows.

With the threat now fleeing, Jacin swiftly secures his weapon and moves with purpose toward his vehicle, where Paco, armed with a rifle, awaits. Dog remains steadfast at the door, barking his vigilance into the night.

"I'm in pursuit of one of the escapees. Get Ahote to the hospital," Jacin yells and slides behind the wheel of his cruiser, the engine growling to life as he maneuvers onto the slick, rain-soaked road and accelerates into the storm's fury. The desert landscape is now a canvas of red mud, the morning storm blurring the horizon into a haze of uncertain shapes.

Ahead, in the distance, the escaping blond-haired man fights against the relentless onslaught of rain and mud. The windshield wipers of his SUV struggle to clear the splattered mess, the cracked glass leaking water onto the interior. The driver's side window is shattered, adding to the disarray within. Despite the adverse conditions, the man presses on; his face is streaked with blood that mingles with the rain, his grip on the steering wheel white-knuckled.

The SUV's instrument panel glows, and the speedometer shows 65 miles per hour. Outside, the vehicle's rear wheels hydroplane, causing it to sway dangerously from side to side. The driver slows, regaining control amid the tumult.

As the storm illuminates the surrounding Mesas with lightning, Jacin's cruiser closes the distance behind the fleeing SUV. The cruiser's headlights and spotlights cast eerie shadows in the downpour. With determination, Jacin reaches for his Beretta, positioning himself for a calculated move.

The man inside the SUV, desperate and erratic, fires two shots through the SUV's rear window, creating gaping holes.

Undeterred, Jacin's cruiser adjusts, pulling alongside the left side of the road. With precision, Jacin maneuvers closer, tapping the SUV's rear bumper, but the fugitive accelerates, veering away.

Jacin's focus intensifies. Pulling up parallel to the rear door of the SUV, he lowers his passenger window, closing the distance even further. With a steady hand, he takes aim and fires into the vehicle, the sound of gunfire mingling with the roar of the storm.

The chase continues, the two vehicles dancing through the tempest, locked in a deadly pursuit amid the relentless fury of the desert storm.

In the midst of a dramatic pursuit, Jacin exchanges gunfire once more with the frantic escapee as the storm rages on. The rain-soaked desert road becomes a battleground, with the SUV struggling to maintain control on the slippery surface. Despite the hazardous conditions, Jacin remains determined, his focus unwavering as he once again closes in on the fleeing vehicle.

Jacin's cruiser veers abruptly as its left wheels leave the pavement, jolting him momentarily. With a firm grip on the steering wheel, he regains control, his resolve unshaken despite the escalating chaos of the pursuit. The storm's relentless assault adds to the challenge, but Jacin presses on, determined to bring the fugitive to justice.

In a tense moment, Jacin finds himself in a dangerous standoff with the suspect. As the SUV maneuvers alongside his cruiser, the two vehicles race in parallel, their paths converging at a lethal crossroads. Jacin, both hands firmly on the wheel, keeps his weapon close at hand, his eyes locked on the driver of the SUV.

Their vehicles hurtle through the storm, rain slashing across the windshield, blurring their vision. The fugitive raises his shotgun, a threatening silhouette against the tempestuous backdrop. In a split-second decision, Jacin jerks the steering wheel hard to the right, aiming his cruiser directly at the SUV.

Within the SUV, the shotgun discharges, but Jacin's maneuver sends the SUV careening into a mudflow, the forces of nature seizing the vehicle and tossing it into a violent spin. The SUV slams into a Mesa, the impact reverberating through the stormy night.

Positioned strategically, Jacin activates his cruiser to a stop, adjusting the searchlight, the beam cutting through the rain-soaked darkness. Illuminated by the harsh light, the blond-haired fugitive is trapped against the steering wheel, his shotgun now pointing dangerously.

With steady aim, Jacin fires, the bullet finding its mark in the man's chest just as the shotgun discharges within the SUV's cabin. The man slumps forward, engulfed by the encroaching mud from the crumbling Mesa.

As the storm rages on, Jacin breathes in the cool, wet air, his pulse slowing with the end of the harrowing pursuit. Reaching for the microphone, he prepares to relay the final chapter of the chase over the crackling radio.

With the threat neutralized, Jacin swiftly proceeds to the hospital for debriefing. Despite the danger and chaos, Jacin remains composed, his resolve unshaken as he navigates the aftermath of the intense confrontation.

At the hospital, Jacin and Paco stand anxiously beside Doctor Wechsler who emerges from the operating room and removes her mask with a sigh of relief. The tension in the air is palpable as they await news of Ranger Ahote's condition.

"He was lucky," Doctor Wechsler explains, her voice calm yet reassuring. "The window and door absorbed most of the shotgun blast. His injuries are mainly from the shattered glass—facial and shoulder lacerations. We've removed all the debris, and he's now in recovery. He should sleep peacefully through the night."

Jacin nods gratefully. "Thank you, Doctor," he replies, his expression reflecting a mix of relief and concern.

Doctor Wechsler nods in acknowledgment before turning back towards the operating room, her footsteps echoing down the corridor.

Paco, standing beside Jacin, shares the details he learned from Ranger Ahote before he was taken into surgery. "He mentioned that when he pulled into the lot, he saw the suspect had opened the trunk of Makia's cruiser and retrieved the shotgun. That's the last thing he remembers."

Jacin absorbs this information silently, his thoughts swirling with the events of the night and the dangerous pursuit. Despite the physical and emotional toll of the events, Jacin remains focused on the task at hand. With one escaped prisoner who has found death in the clutches of a crumbling Mesa, his attention returns to the murder of the two men at Mesa Two and the mysterious method of their demise.

As Jacin and Paco leave the hospital, the night promises that the storm is moving east, but the tension lingers in the cool, damp air. Reflecting on the day's events, Jacin is mindful of the challenges ahead, knowing that the pursuit of truth and justice will require untiring determination to unravel the lingering questions. Who were these two strangers found dead on the cliff's side on Hopi land? How did they die, and what brought their death to the shadows of the towering ancient Mesa Two? Were they drug mules escaping the deadly Mexican coyotes or something at this point unexplainable?

The rain has dwindled to a drizzle as they approach Jacin's battered cruiser in the emergency parking lot adjacent to a Ranger Jeep Wrangler Rubicon. Paco surveys the damage, walking around the mud-covered vehicle with a mixture of curiosity and concern.

"What the hell happened out there?" Paco asks, his voice laced with urgency.

"The man didn't quite grasp gravity. He's now part of a Mesa just outside the southwestern Navajo Nation line," Jacin responds solemnly.

"Dead?" Paco inquires.

"Buried in mud and Mesa rock," Jacin confirms.

"Did you notify DPS?" Paco questions further.

"No. I called the Flagstaff State Police. It's a State and FBI problem," Jacin explains.

Paco peers through the side window of the cruiser, observing the aftermath of the intense pursuit.

"Just across the line," Paco notes.

"About 50 feet. Where's Dog?" Jacin asks, looking around.

"He fell asleep in the jeep," Paco chuckles lightly.

"I think it's best if you drive us home," Jacin decides.

They make their way to the nearby Jeep Wrangler, and Paco unlocks the doors. Dog perks up with excitement as Jacin approaches.

"If Kele sees that cruis—" Paco begins, but Jacin cuts him off abruptly.

"Not a word about it... understand?" Jacin's tone brooks no argument.

"So I would guess she does not know about you popping Jesse James at the bank yesterday?" Paco asks.

"No! I'll tell her when the time is right," Jacin replies firmly.

Paco gets on the driver's side and starts the jeep. They pull out into the wet night, the heat mist hanging in the air.

"I'll send a truck to pick it up tomorrow," Paco agrees, acknowledging the necessity of handling the cruiser.

"Tell Flagstaff they may need a bulldozer for the SUV," Jacin adds, his thoughts already moving forward.

Jacin settles into the passenger's side of the jeep, his gaze reflecting the weight of the day's events. He knows the road ahead will demand a planned relationship with Winslow's PD Lieutenant Robert (Robb) Parker. Paco takes the driver's seat, starts the engine, and pulls out into the misty night. The heat of the desert envelops them as they journey home, Dog happily sleeping by Jacin's side.

Chapter 4: What Could Happen?

As the evening settles over the Arizona desert, Jacin, Paco, and Dog return to Jacin's small adobe house, seeking solace after the intensity of the day's events. The scent of rain continues to linger in the air as they enter, greeted by the warmth of home.

Jacin leads the way inside with Paco trailing behind, while Dog pauses at the screen door before wandering off to find his spot in the barn. "You staying for dinner?" Jacin offers.

"That depends," Paco replies.

Inside, Kele emerges from the kitchen, her gaze immediately falling on the muddy boots of the two men. "Wipe your muddy boots, both of you," she instructs, her tone firm but loving. Upon closer inspection, she added, "In fact, take your boots off. You both look terrible. Jacin, take the shirt off and give it to me, and go wash your hands and face."

They take their boots off, and Jacin slips out of the wet shirt to reveal a tight-fitting white tee shirt. Meanwhile, Paco walks to the dinner table and sits down, wiping his hands with a napkin.

Kele busies herself to set the table, and her concern is evident in her actions. "Why did you let me sleep this morning? You didn't even leave me a note," she questions from the kitchen, her voice tinged with worry.

"We had an agreement. When you put that gun on, you tell me where you're going," Kele states.

"What if something happened to you out there...?!" Kele's concern escalates, and her worry for Jacin becomes palpable.

"What could happen?" Paco interjects, attempting to diffuse the tension with a touch of humour.

Giving a disapproving look to Paco, "You needed your rest," Jacin reassures Kele, his voice carrying a soothing undertone.

"Is that Sal's truck out there?" Jacin's attention shifts to the vehicle parked outside, his curiosity piqued. Kele responds, "I called Sal to look at the wiring in the barn."

With dinner served and Sal's arrival announced by a knock at the door, the atmosphere at the table becomes more relaxed.

"What did you find out there?" Jacin directs the question to Sal and his curiosity about the reason for the call.

"The wires going to the box somehow loosened, probably because of the storm. Could have caused a fire," Sal reports, his voice tinged with concern.

"Good thing I called you," Kele remarks, her gratitude evident in her tone.

"How's your mother doing?" Jacin inquires, his concern for Sal's family evident in his voice.

"She's fine. Tonight is the 'Hopi Mothers for Better Schools' meeting," Sal shares, his voice carrying a note of pride.

Sal's presence adds to the sense of camaraderie, his easy familiarity with Jacin and Paco speaking to their shared history. Despite the seriousness of their professions, they find comfort in each other's company, sharing stories and laughter about their college days over the dinner table.

"Ohh, that's right, I forgot," Kele acknowledges, her memory jogged by Sal's reminder.

"What's it like working for the Government? They pay you well," Kele probes, his curiosity piqued by Sal's profession.

"How much do they pay you?" Paco inquires.

"You know Paco, courtesy is as much a mark of a gentleman as courage itself," Sal comments, his observation directed at Paco. Then, looking at Jacin, he asks, "You involved in the prison break?" "DPS is on it," Jacin confirms, his voice carrying a note of authority.

"The Department of Public Safety, of course... is in CHARGE!!!" Paco adds, his sarcasm evident in his tone.

Jacin is ignoring Paco's statement. "They asked me to investigate a crime scene up at Mesa Two." Kele purposely moves the subject away from the dinner table to whatever crime occurred at the Mesa and looks to Sal. "You had mentioned you were working on something up there?"

Sal, understanding the hint, responds, "The Governor has had me working on designing a new power grid at Mesa Two for nearly a year now. I have heard a lot of strange stories about those Mesas."

"They sure could use the convenience of reliable electricity in their homes," Jacin agrees, his voice thoughtful.

As the conversation opens on the need for improvement in the Hopi territory, Jacin receives a phone call that cuts their meal short.

"Hello... Now?... Understood... On my way," Jacin's voice is brisk as he concludes the call.

He takes a shirt from the closet, slips on his boots, and prepares to leave.

"We've got to go," Jacin announces, his tone urgent.

"Jacin, your dinner!" Kele's concern for Jacin's well-being is evident in her voice.

"What is it?" Paco inquires, his curiosity piqued by Jacin's sudden departure.

"Doc Torrey needs to see us; we have to go to Winslow," Jacin says.

As Jacin and Paco prepare to leave, Jacin exchanges final words with Sal. "Thanks for taking care of the electrical wires in the barn. Talk tomorrow."

"Drive safe," Kele urges, her voice tinged with concern for Jacin's safety.

Kele's understanding and support shine through as she places her hand on his shoulder and fixes his shirt collar, her love and concern evident as she follows him to the door. She looks up at Jacin, who leans down and kisses her on the forehead and walks out, followed by Paco as they head out into the night, ready to face whatever challenges await them beyond the safety of home.

Chapter 5: Unexplained Murders Lead to a Hypothesis

Jacin, still with the day's events on his mind, remains silent as he makes his way through the desert's misty heat mingling with the night air to the Winslow Hospital Morgue. The air carries a faint, clean, fresh after-rain smell as they descend several steps and enter the hallway leading to the autopsy room.

"Oh yes, the distinctive odor of decaying bodies. I think I smell something else," Paco remarks, his tone tinged with sarcasm.

"Keep your mouth shut in there, and don't get into it with Robb. Hear me?" Jacin advises sternly.

"He is such an asshole," Paco mutters under his breath.

"Not a word," Jacin insists firmly.

They step into the autopsy room to find the bodies of Mesa Two, now naked and partly covered, lying on the autopsy tables. Dr. Torrey, a slim, studious gentleman in his early 50s wearing a lab coat over a yellow dress shirt and a green tie, stands beside

Lieutenant Robert Parker (Robb) from Winslow PD, who is medium-height and well-built, dressed in a blue dress shirt and matching khakis. Both men are engrossed in examining some X-rays.

"Doc, Robb, what do we have?" Jacin inquires, stepping closer to the tables for a better look.

"Jacin, sorry to bring you out this late, but I told the Lieutenant you had to see this," Dr. Torrey begins.

"Both these guys have a hole in the base of their heads, and someone took a carving knife to them, and their index fingers have been cut off," Robb interjects bluntly.

Looking at Dr. Torrey, Jacin asks, "Did you recover the bullet?"

"A bullet did not make the incursion," Dr. Torrey responds, turning to an X-ray screen showing a detailed negative image.

Paco crouches down to inspect the perfectly round holes closely.

"I took a lot of close-ups of it. Looked like a bullet wound to me," Paco remarks, examining the holes.

"Normally, I would not have bothered with much of an autopsy, but something did not feel right," Dr. Torrey explains, turning on a separate viewing screen with another X-ray image.

"Whoever did this removed exactly a four-inch core of what may have been flesh, muscle, and brain matter from both nicks," Dr. Torrey continues.

"Were they alive or dead at the time of removing the core?" Paco questions, his curiosity piqued.

"I'm not sure if something was removed or inserted. I do believe they were alive for a time," Dr. Torrey responds thoughtfully.

"Then that was the cause of death," Robb concludes matter-of-factly.

"Not necessarily. Simply put, I believe that both men had Auto Immune System (AIS), and the heart just stopped beating," Dr. Torrey clarifies.

"Acute Arthritis?" Jacin queries, seeking clarification.

"I would guess, at this point, a very rare form of AIS causing immense internal swelling, resulting in the heart ceasing to function," Dr. Torrey explains, his demeanor serious.

As Jacin absorbs this information, his mind races with the implications of these findings. He realizes that their investigation has taken a sudden and unexpected turn. The mystery deepens, and the pursuit of truth grows more complex with each revelation.

"Did the hole in his neck kill him or bring on the heart attack?" Robb asks, his tone weighted with the gravity of the situation.

"I can't answer that as of yet," Dr. Torrey replies thoughtfully.

"Whoever did this redressed them in these misfitting old clothes to make it appear that they might be border crossing illegals," Jacin observes, his mind racing with possibilities.

"Possibly," Dr. Torrey concedes, considering the implications.

"Any identification on them?" Paco inquires, seeking further clarity.

"Nothing. I instructed the Doc to pull prints despite the fingertips being burned. However, I believe the lab can still retrieve some information from them," Robb responds, shedding light on the investigation's progress.

"Not unusual... If they were drug mules. So, Doc, did they die of a heart attack, or was it murder?" Jacin presses, seeking definitive answers.

"I also took additional blood and brain tissue samples and rushed them to the lab. Should have that answer tomorrow," Dr. Torrey assures, his dedication evident.

"Okay. You call me just as soon as you have the results in," Robb requests, emphasizing the urgency of the matter.

"You'll be the first to know right after I call Jacin. We don't know if drugs were involved. If not, since the bodies were found on Indian land, Jacin would be the lead on this," Dr. Torrey explains, signalling the shifting dynamics of the investigation.

As Doc Torrey carries a tray over to the sink and winks at Paco, Jacin turns to Robb.

"Looks like we're going to be working on this one together," Jacin remarks, acknowledging the necessity of collaboration despite any personal reservations.

The expression on Robb's face shows clear displeasure with the situation, his demeanor reflecting the weight of the investigation's implications.

"One last thing," Doc Torrey interjects before Robb can voice his concerns. "The deep cuts were..."

"Someone sliced them both up badly. Why?" Robb interrupts, his voice tinged with frustration.

"Upon death, the perpetrator, using a scalpel, I would assume, shaved about five inches long by about one-quarter of an inch deep piece from various matching parts of both bodies," Doc Torrey elaborates, revealing another disturbing detail.

"Like carving a turkey," Paco remarks grimly, drawing a chilling comparison.

"Precisely," Doc Torrey confirms, his expression grave.

As the trio leaves the morgue and walks to their cars, the clouded sky mirrors the uncertainty that looms over the investigation. The abnormal blood results, the precision of the wounds, and the looming question of the cause of death deepen the shadows cast by the mysterious deaths.

"This goes beyond our usual caseload, Robb. It's like we've stepped into a world where the rules are different,"

Jacin emphasizes, his voice laden with the weight of the unknown.

Lieutenant Parker nods thoughtfully, absorbing the gravity of Jacin's words. "Are you thinking this might be linked to some sort of a new Columbia ritualistic murder gang imported to deal with runaways? That, my friend, can lead to drug-unrelated killings."

"That is not exactly what I was thinking, but it's a possibility. The bodies were found on Indian land, and for now, we've agreed to put it under my jurisdiction, but we need to tread carefully and work together. This is no ordinary case," Jacin warns, his voice tinged with concern. Too many unanswered questions to call it anything other than murder by an unknown predator.

The lieutenant sighs, realizing the complexity of the situation. "Alright, Jacin. We'll collaborate, but we need to keep this under wraps. If there's something bigger at play, we don't want to tip our hand too soon to many."

Crimes like these can easily give way to panic and fear. And we have had enough of that in the past couple of years. Lieutenant Parker is a man who has proven over time that he has never embraced the old way of the Hopi people. He looks at crime with a more simplistic eye and finds a logical answer to the motive, the course of action, and the obvious clues and evidence. At this point, the crime may have been committed to stop the theft of legal drugs. The hint of a Columbia ritualistic murder gang imported to deal with runaways fulfilled his need for motive and execution of the act.

On the other hand, Jacin's deep tribal heritage whispered of something profound, resonating beyond the surface of these murders on Navajo land. The weight of ancestral knowledge and spiritual ties imbued the investigation with an eerie significance, hinting at connections that transcended mere mortal understanding.

The morning brings clear blue skies as Jacin enters the office and is greeted by Ranger Karen Masawepimana, Jacin's administrative deputy.

"Good morning, Lieutenant Yazzie," Karen says warmly, handing Jacin a stack of messages.

Jacin glances at the messages before turning to Karen with a thoughtful expression. "Did you read the final Coroner's report that came in yesterday?"

"Yes, and I am beginning to believe that this is more than just a border drug smugglers incident," Karen replies, her tone serious.

Jacin takes a seat, clearly interested in what Karen has discovered from the report.

"There are too many questions that don't tie the murders to any Colombian ritualistic machete-wielding murder gang that I have been able to find," Karen explains.

"They were not tortured. The flesh wounds occurred after the heart stopped beating. The shaft at the base of their skulls was obviously made by some sort of device either inserted or retrieved while they were alive. According to Doc Torrey, they may have actually died from some sort of congenital heart failure brought on by AIS. It does not add up to murder by some Colombian nut case," She continues.

"I'm afraid that was exactly what Doc Torrey was trying not to say in front of Robb," Jacin remarks. "I found the Colombian idea a convenient answer to prevent a witch hunt for a killer whose purpose was unrelated to drugs but rather something more clandestine."

"To me, as I said, there are just too many questions and not enough logical answers," Karen agrees.

"You're right. Why the cliff ledge on Mesa Two? That just doesn't make sense. As far as I can tell, they were not of any tribal family. Doc Torrey has listed their origin as Caucasian."

"For now, it's best to continue to list the crime as another border killing," Jacin decides, standing up and looking over his messages. "Did you send Makia to talk to Gray Wolf about the wild dogs?"

Karen answers with a hint of a smile. "Makia went out there and helped mend the fences around the chicken coop. I think he just needed someone to help him. You know he's alone out there since his son and wife died."

Jacin nods as he starts for his office, pausing before leaving. "Any word on the other escapee?"

"I put a full report on your desk. A camper was killed, and his vehicle was taken. They have now brought in some Navajo trackers," Karen reports.

"They should have done that on day one," Jacin remarks with a hint of frustration. "I talked to Lieutenant Parker this morning, and we agreed that until Dr. Torrey gets the test back later today, there is not a whole lot more we can do." "Continue your research on AIS, give a call to the Hopi library, and ask if there is any significance to the Mesa cliffs around Mesa Two." " I am going to pick up Paco and talk to a friend with the border patrol."

Chapter 6: Murder At Mesa Crater

The misty early morning wind carries an air of mystery as Sal and another man, both dressed in jeans, orange worker's vests, and hard hats, approach the steel cover of the power vault near the Crater Museum. Sal, carrying a large, rolled-up schematic, unrolls it as they stop by the vault, preparing to review the plans.

"What the hell is this?" the other man suddenly exclaims, pointing to something on the vault doors.

Sal glances down to see what caught the man's attention. "Someone cut the lock on the vault clean through," he observes, with no burn marks around the edges of the lock.

Taking a penlight from his vest, Sal kneels and opens one of the steel covers, shining the light down into the 13' long x 9' wide x 7'.6" tall vault room below. After a moment's inspection, he closes the cover and looks back at his companion.

"A body," Sal confirms.

"Dead?" the man asks, his tone edged with concern.

"Tell the curator to close off the steps and platform down here," Sal instructs firmly. "Head back to the plant and not a word about this."

The man nods and quickly departs. Moments later, Jacin arrives at the gate in his cruiser, accompanied by Paco, who wears a ranger shirt and a gun belt.

"Go up and make sure they have closed off all entrances to the museum and other buildings," Jacin directs Paco.

Paco acknowledges the order and heads toward the main gate. Meanwhile, Sal waits for Jacin at the bottom of the steps leading to the visitor center of the crater site.

"Morning, Sal," Jacin greets as he approaches.

"It's in the electrical vault. This way. I sent my partner back to the plant," Sal informs Jacin.

Leading the way, Sal guides Jacin to an area near the side of the visitor center where the electrical vault is located. He points to the vault covers, drawing Jacin's attention.

"Someone cut through the lock with some kind of torch and made a hole in the three-foot thick cement wall below," Sal explains, preparing to open the cover.

Sal lifts the cover and shines his light inside, revealing the body within. Jacin crouches down to get a closer look.

"Did you go down there?" Jacin asks cautiously.

"No. By the look of the body, he was electrocuted. I don't think you should go down there until I check it out," Sal advises, his tone grave.

Jacin peers into the dimly lit vault, his eyes adjusting to the shadows. "Let me see your light," he requests, and Sal obliges by handing him a pen light. The narrow beam illuminates the compact 13' long x 9' wide x 7'.6" tall vault room space of the Volt interior. Jacin directs the light toward a hole in the side wall and then to the various dials, switches, and electrical cables. Finally, it settles on the back of a man's head, where a bloody hole is just visible at the base of his neck.

Turning to Paco, who has just arrived, Jacin's tone is urgent. "Call Robb and Doc Torrey," he instructs.

Paco promptly hands Jacin a tablet. "Thought you might need this. What's down there?" Paco inquires.

"A body with a hole in the neck," Jacin responds succinctly.

"Spooky!" Paco remarks before exiting the scene.

Sal takes the penlight and carefully descends the ladder into the vault. There's a tense beat before Jacin calls out to him, concerned. "Is it safe to come down?"

"Hold on," Sal replies from below. "He's fried, and the hole is a clean cut in five inches of cement. I'm coming up." Soon, Sal emerges from the vault. "It's okay to go down," he confirms. "Just don't touch anything."

Jacin gives him a look and wastes no time climbing into the vault, immediately pulling out the tablet to capture the scene.

"Strange wound at the base of the man's head," Sal notes.

"Yeah, same as the bodies we found at Mesa Two," Jacin confirms as he exits the vault.

Meanwhile, Paco returns, peering down into the vault with curiosity. "Did you reach Robb?" Jacin questions him.

"The asshole was in a county helicopter, headed back from picking up the results of Doc's tests. They're bringing it here. I also called Doc," Paco reports.

"I didn't think he would wait for them to get it to Doc," Jacin remarks thoughtfully.

"Oh. I did call it into the DPS, but they transferred it to you," Sal interjects.

"That's right. You're a government man now, and you follow the system," Paco teases.

"Back off, Paco, this is state land; he didn't have a choice," Jacin defends.

"On Navaho dirt," Paco adds.

Jacin, addressing Sal, continues, "DPS force is still at the Crayon."

"The prison escape?" Sal seeks confirmation.

Paco, hearing the approach of a helicopter, turns towards the sound.

Outside in the parking lot, a county helicopter maneuvers around and touches down.

"He circled so he could make his entrance over the crater. What an ass!" Paco comments with disdain.

Jacin hands Paco the tablet. "Don't start on him," Jacin cautions.

Sal agrees with Paco's assessment. "Paco's right. You know Robb's been that way since college; he's just naturally annoying at times. He hasn't changed."

Paco responds with a smile and a high-five to Sal.

Outside at the Crater Hillside, a mysterious figure stands behind one of the crater's spyglass units, their face concealed by the long device. Towering Mesas loom in the background. The identity of the man remains an intriguing question.

Through the spyglass, we see Robb joining Paco, Jacin, and Sal at the vault. Robb enters the scene just as the view through the spyglass times out and goes blank.

Inside a museum restaurant in the afternoon, Jacin, Paco, Sal, Doc Torrey, and Robb gather around a table, the restaurant empty save for them. Through the window, two men from the morgue wheel a body bag past.

Doc Torrey takes a locked pouch from Robb, unlocks it with a key, and retrieves files from inside. He reads the report and then hands it to Jacin, passing another report to Robb.

"The blood from both men did have some irregularities in their cell count," Doc Torrey explains as Jacin examines the report and passes it on to Robb.

"The white blood cells are a mixture of known and unknown substances," Doc Torrey elaborates.

"What the hell does that mean, known and unknown?" Robb, perplexed, demands answers.

"They were not human cells," Sal interjects.

"Animal or what?" Robb presses.

"No. Unknown shows that science has not yet found or classified the cell's prominent content," Doc Torrey clarifies.

Paco expresses disbelief. "Are you telling us that these cells are from some unknown creature?"

"No. I am merely saying science does not know what the substance is," Doc Torrey asserts.

Jacin shifts the focus, "What about the tissue samples?"

"Same results," Doc Torrey replies. "And they confirmed my suspicions; they each had a rare case of ISA... and the fluid-based swelling basically crushed the heart."

Jacin turns to Robb with another query. "Robb, was your lab able to identify the two men from the prints?"

"First, the FBI office in Phoenix called and blocked any further testing," Robb explains. "After some haggling, they finally told me both men worked for a government agency."

"Did they tell you which agency?" Jacin probes.

"No, I thought they may be DEA agents, but they said they had ultra-top-secret clearance," Robb responds before handing over the report to Jacin for inspection. Jacin reviews it briefly and then passes it to Sal.

Paco, eager for answers, presses, "Well, what does it say?"

The conversation buzzes with tension and intrigue as the group unravels the mysteries surrounding the strange findings and their implications for the unidentified men and the government agency involved.

Sal drops a bombshell. "One of them was Homer Penny, and the other was Gerry Winfield."

Paco, eager for more details, asks, "And?"

Robb explains, "I called a buddy in the Washington office, and an hour later, I got the yellow sheet and a warning this could turn dark." Jacin promptly retrieves the yellow sheet from his file.

"What does it say?" Paco urges.

"Homer was born in 1900 and died on November 13th, 1947. Gerry Winfield was born in 1910 and died November 13th, 1947," Jacin reads aloud before handing the report to Paco.

"That would make them over a hundred years old," Paco remarks, astonished.

"Bullshit. Those corpses didn't look fifty, let alone a hundred," Robb protests.

"Are you sure the Feds are not putting you on, Robb?" Paco questions skeptically.

"No! But there must be something wrong with the prints I sent in," Robb insists.

"Yes, they were probably from a couple of spooks who were still collecting their government pensions," Paco quips.

"Impossible! It's not... conceivable!" Robb exclaims, clearly shaken.

Jacin turns to Doc Torrey, seeking more insights. "Was there anything further from your tests?"

Doc Torrey nods. "Yes. The brain matter within the holes had become aggravated by some continuous metallic substance, which is an unknown material."

"So it was not something stabbed into his neck and had been there for a time," Jacin deduces.

"Yes, that's the prognosis from the lab. It is basically what I had surmised," Doc Torrey confirms.

Robb interjects with another pressing question. "I still want to know if they died of a heart attack induced by the hole in the neck."

"That is a little simplified, but I'll answer that after I've had a chance to take a closer look at these reports," Doc Torrey replies.

Jacin redirects the conversation, "Do we know any more about how they supposedly died in 1947?"

"Yes. This morning, after Robb called me about the FBI file, I checked online about the date November 13th, 1947," Doc Torrey reveals, handing a document to Jacin. Before Jacin can take it, Robb snatches it away.

"This is more bullshit! That's impossible!" Robb exclaims in disbelief.

Paco intervenes, swiftly taking the document from Robb and passing it to Jacin. Jacin studies it briefly before handing it to Paco.

"On August 13th, 1947, a military DC4 left Fort Knox, Kentucky at five in the morning and had seven passengers, two MPs, a pilot, and co-pilot," Jacin recites.

"The cargo was over thirty million in gold bars and bagged gold coins. Destination San Francisco," Paco adds.

"It never made it but crashed in the desert on the Navaho Reservation," Sal chimes in.

"Doc, do you have any explanation of how we have two, maybe three dead people who have been walking around for over seventy-five years?" Jacin asks, bewildered.

"It's bullshit... The dates are a coincidence," Robb insists.

"If something was inserted in that hole and somehow attached to the spinal cord, it could control the aging process and other body functions. I have read several studies," Doc Torrey hypothesizes, shedding light on the baffling situation.

Robb's interruption slices through the speculative air. "That science fiction crap?!"

Sal counters, unfazed. "No, Doc is right. NASA scientists have been exploring the idea for years. If they could place an astronaut in some form of sustainable sleep and travel them for fifty or more years at light speed, we could reach into the far universe."

Paco chimes in with his theory. "Maybe these guys were part of some kind of government scientific experiment, and whatever they were exposed to caused the AIS and also slowed the aging process."

Robb dismisses the notion outright. "Like I said, science fiction. This is nothing more than some crazy, hopped-up, Columbian serial killer."

Jacin redirects the conversation, emphasizing the need for action. "Whatever this is, we need to stop him or her before anyone else is killed, no matter how old they are."

Doc Torrey takes charge of the next steps. "I am going to run further tests this afternoon, and for now, keep the results between us."

"Agreed," Jacin confirms. "This one was a possible electrical accident."

Lieutenant Parker, understanding the gravity of the situation, cautiously agrees to continued collaboration. "Alright, Jacin. We'll continue to collaborate. If there's any chance these murders lead to something bigger at play, then I may take your theories more seriously."

Paco, sensing the need to disengage, stands and redirects attention away from Robb. "Robby, I think your helicopter pilot is late for his lunch..."

Robb remains seated, voicing his perspective with finality. "You're all nuts. Over a thousand migrant bodies have been found from the Arizona border north just this year. As I said, I'm treating this like any other serial killing. Doc, I want a report on this latest body in the morning."

Meanwhile, Jacin, Sal, and Paco begin to walk away, clearly disregarding Robb's skepticism.

Doc Torrey pauses briefly, offering a crucial piece of advice. "I will, but strongly advise you, leave out the blood results on your reports. I'll continue to do the blood work myself. Don't rush to let this get out."

With that, Doc Torrey follows the others, leaving Robb to ponder the unfolding mysteries on his own.

Each, in their own way, would now navigate the intricate web of shadows enshrouding the investigation, each revelation tightening the mystery and hinting at a larger, more ominous design. In Lieutenant Parker's mind, the possibility of a link to a new border drug syndicate elevated the stakes, casting these strange murders into the nexus of a clandestine world.

Jacin, on the other hand, would embark on a relentless pursuit of truth, navigating the murky depths of an underworld where ancient Hopi rituals and modern crime converged. As he delves deeper, the shadows grow denser, obscuring the boundaries between light and darkness, revealing only fleeting glimpses of the sinister forces at play. Each step forward unravels a thread of intrigue, leading Jacin closer to the heart of a mystery that defies conventional explanations. A mystery tied to a military aircraft that found its way to the Navaho land and death nearly 80 years ago.

Chapter 7: The Collector

Jacin's small adobe house stands quietly in the early evening light. Jacin and Paco arrive, closely followed by Sal's van.

Inside Jacin's home, they all enter together. Kele's voice cuts through the air, "Take your shoes off." They comply, removing their shoes and making their way to the dinner table before sitting down. Kele moves into the kitchen, her presence felt even when unseen.

From the kitchen, Kele calls out, "You boys hungry? I can make you something."

Jacin responds, "It was late, and we stopped and had something on the way. Thought you would be in bed by now."

"I was getting Mato's room ready. He will be home tomorrow," Kele explains.

Paco, intrigued by the offer of food, asks, "If we were to eat, what were you thinking of serving?"

Kele's voice rings out again, "Left-over chicken tacos and beans."

"Sounds good," Paco replies enthusiastically.

"Anyone else?" Kele asks.

Jacin, now focused on his open laptop, shakes his head, signalling no. Sal also declines, "No, thank you."

Jacin's curiosity gets the better of him. "I'm curious. Why the vault?" he asks Sal.

Sal shakes his head, "I have no idea. I checked it out before placing a new lock on it. Beside the hole in the wall, everything was in place."

"Why the hole? What was behind the vault wall?" Jacin probes further.

"I have a set of vault plans in the truck," Sal replies, getting up and heading outside.

Paco turns to Jacin, "What are you thinking, boss?"

"Not sure yet," Jacin admits.

Outside, Sal opens the door of his van and retrieves the rolled-up schematics. He pauses, glancing back at the barn before heading back inside the house.

Re-entering, Sal hands the schematics to Jacin, who places them beside his laptop. Jacin's eyes scan the computer screen.

"Here it is, August 13th, 1947. This article says there were six, not seven, passengers and two MPs aboard when it crashed. The bodies were nothing but ashes, no survivors. No sign of the gold. They blamed pilot error, hijackers, even the Las Vegas mafia."

Paco muses, "You think the gold was in a mine where the vault is located?"

"Maybe... And the other locations?" Jacin ponders aloud.

Sal interrupts, "Hold on, I have to check something out." He leaves once again, heading to his van. Then, he makes his way to the barn, where he inspects the wiring he had fixed earlier. He switches on the light. Suddenly, sparks fly from the wall where the wires lead to the house. A fire flares up, rapidly advancing towards the house.

Sal rushes back to the van and grabs an electric fire extinguisher. With urgency, he sprays the wires, successfully stopping the flames just outside the house.

Jacin rushes out of the house, followed closely by Kele and Dog. Sal, standing near the recently extinguished wires, looks up at them, his face grim. "Someone had plans on burning your house down," he says.

Kele gasps, "Oh my God, Jacin!"

Sal nods, "Something bothered me when I fixed those wires yesterday."

Paco emerges from the house, a half-eaten taco in his hand. "Oh shit!" he exclaims, taking in the scene.

Jacin, trying to piece things together, murmurs, "A warning? I think we'll call it a night. Leave me the jeep, Sal. Can you take Paco home?"

Sal hesitates, "First, I'd better run a new line and clean up the wiring."

Paco, still chewing, suggests, "And I should stay with Gah, and the two of us sleep in the barn with my Winchester 44."

Jacin shakes his head, "No. Go home. I got his message. Leave it tonight, Sal."

"Are you sure?" Sal asks, looking concerned.

Jacin wraps an arm around Kele, reassuring her. "Yes. I'll switch on the generator. Sal, get on it first thing tomorrow."

Sal nods, accepting the decision.

***

The morning light reveals the interior of a city morgue. Jacin and Paco walk into the stark autopsy room where Doc Torrey is just finishing up an examination. Stepping away from the table, he removes his plastic mask and gloves and then walks to the sink to wash his hands.

"Morning, Doc," Jacin greets him.

Paco sets down a small bag on a nearby counter, adding, "Morning, Doc. Got you one of those fancy coffees."

Doc Torrey dries his hands and looks into the bag, a smile of appreciation crossing his face. "Good morning, gentlemen. I do not know what they put in these things, but they are addictive."

He pulls out the large cup from the bag, clearly grateful. "Thanks, Paco. I need it. I've been up all night."

Doc Torrey, still holding his coffee, starts, "I received a call from Flagstaff about the body you sent over there."

Jacin looks curious. "The escaped convict dropped by my office to pick up a weapon and a cruiser."

Doc nods. "They said he was buried in a mesa on 99."

Jacin explains, "Figured I'd take the heat off this office. You said you found something you wanted us to see before Robby got here."

"First, look at this," Doc says, handing Jacin a silicone cast of a cylinder about three inches long and slightly thicker than a pencil.

Jacin examines it closely. "Strange prongs or needles," he observes, then passes it to Paco.

Doc continues, "Prongs are closer to what they represent. Sal was right yesterday. Some kind of device most likely to control thought and aging."

Paco looks skeptical. "This little tube?"

Doc nods. "Yes. My guess is someone inserted these into the body and surgically connected them to the spinal cord and brain. Hell of a procedure."

Jacin frowns, pondering the implications. "Our technology, or..."

Doc interrupts, "I can't answer that, but the blood tests I did myself last night tell me the blood is definitely not completely human."

Paco is stunned. "These guys were aliens."

"Maybe," Jacin says thoughtfully, "but I don't think it's that simple."

Doc clarifies, "Yes. There is no question that the deceased were human, at least at one time. I did not send in these tests or further details."

Jacin asks, "Do we know anything more about this third victim?"

Doc nods. "Well, I did some more digging on a hunch. An old friend I know in Phoenix collects historical newspapers. I gave him a call and asked if he had any Arizona articles about the DC4 that crashed here in '47. He sent this to me this morning."

Doc turns on a lightbox, illuminating pictures from an old, yellowed newspaper showing five of the seven passengers.

Paco reads aloud, "According to this article, it was seven passengers."

Doc points out the images. "It's a little fuzzy, but here are the first two: Dr. Gerry Winfield and Dr. Homer Kyle...both PhDs."

He then points to another image. "This one is the man on the table. Dr. Malcolm Fisher, U.S. Government, CPA."

Doc enlarges the last two photographs. Paco squints at them. "A woman was also aboard. Dr. Diana Richards, PhD. All but Malcolm were American nuclear physicists. There were no photos of the other two."

Paco walks over to the table and pulls down the sheet, revealing the top of the man's head and exposing the brain. Paco, visibly disturbed, puts the sheet back over the exposed brain. "That was not a good idea," he mutters.

Doc Torrey insists, "Trust me. It is the same man in this photograph."

Jacin processes the information. "So, possibly one of these others will be the next victim or killer."

Doc nods. "I made a copy of the photographs for you."

"What are you going to tell Robb?" Jacin asks.

Doc replies, "He will bring whatever he has heard from the Feds, who are more than a little curious about what we found."

Paco, handing the mold back to Doc, says, "This as well."

Doc passes it to Jacin. "Robb said it was all science fiction, so why don't you keep it for now?"

"Thanks," Jacin responds.

Doc continues, "I have a theory about the devices. Mind you; it is just a theory. An entity implanted them in these men, not of our species."

Jacin is intrigued. "Doc, then you are suggesting an alien from..."

Doc cuts him off, "Yes. A foreign species. I know it sounds crazy, but I believe that their entire individual existence is within each tiny cylinder. To survive in this world, they transferred the very essence of their species in order to take possession of these bodies."

Paco shakes his head, "Robb's going to love that."

Jacin adds, "And that is one reason why the Feds are all over this. Still doesn't answer why the scientists were aboard the plane."

Doc interjects, "Robb called and said he was going to be delayed."

Jacin becomes serious. "Everything we have discussed this morning goes no further than the three of us. Understand?"

Doc and Paco agree.

Doc then says, "There's one more thing. The first two bodies have changed."

He leads Jacin and Paco to the wall where the cold storage drawers containing the bodies are kept. He opens one and pulls back the sheet.

Paco exclaims, "Oh shit! Their bodies have deflated."

Doc nods. "That is certainly one way of putting it. The bodies have started an accelerated decomposition and entered the early stages of decay."

Jacin observes, "They're showing their actual age."

Doc agrees, "Precisely."

Chapter 8: Hopi Spirits

The morning sun casts a warm glow through the windows of the Hopi Tribe Police Ranger's office. Karen sits behind her receptionist's desk, poised and efficient as always. As Jacin and Paco enter, Karen greets them with a smile.

"Good morning, Lieutenant Yazzie, Ranger Nez. Sahale Johnson is waiting for you in your office, and we have a new back door unpainted but installed," Karen announces.

Jacin hands Karen a notebook and says, "I'm expecting a call from Lieutenant Robb Parker. Here are the notes on yesterday's killing. Take a look at them and let me know what you think now. You're dead on about your feeling that these were not Columbian gang killings."

Karen nods in acknowledgment. "I will have it for you this afternoon."

"Copy the report and your notes to Doc Torrey and Lieutenant Parker. But keep my notes from Parker; stay with the Columbians," Jacin instructs.

"Understood," Karen replies.

Jacin proceeds into his office, where Sal has already arranged a series of maps on the wall. Meanwhile, Paco engages in conversation with Karen at the front desk.

"Good morning," Sal announces as Jacin enters.

"I rewired the house and barn this morning," he continues. "Maybe I am wrong, but I don't believe it was the storm."

"Interesting, thanks, Pal," Jacin replies and decides to let it go for now as he calls out to Paco in the front office, "Paco, leave Karen to her work and get in here."

"What did Torrey say about this latest killing?" Sal inquires.

Jacin purposely holds back certain details, replying, "The body has the same injuries as the first two."

While the two are busy discussing the latest killings, Paco enters the room. He tries to catch the tail end of the conversation but chooses to remain silent about the meeting with Doc Torrey.

"After last night, I got to thinking. we were on the right tract. If you look at this 1946 geography map, I have marked the registered mines from Winslow to the crater," Sal says, laying out his thoughts.

"Back then, they were poking holes in the ground all over the area," Paco adds.

"I think I know where you're going with this," Jacin remarks, sensing Sal's train of thought.

"The DC4 is carrying over thirty million in gold bars and coins to be theoretically delivered to the mint in San Francisco. Why the gold? Why a military escort?" Sal questions.

"I haven't found anything to explain it, or why the scientist?" Jacin replies.

"In 1946, the government enacted the Bretton Woods System, allowing other governments to sell their gold to the United States at $35.00 an ounce," Sal offers, providing historical context.

"I think the spot price today is about $1,800.00 an ounce," Jacin notes.

"The two articles we have found say they never located the gold," Paco adds.

"So where do you hide 30 million in gold on a stormy desert night?" Jacin muses.

"Exactly. The plane crashed somewhere around here," Sal points to a position on the map.

"That is at the edge of the Navajo Reservation," Jacin observes.

"And where are the points where we find the bodies?" Paco asks.

"Here is the old shed and a mine above the crater," Sal replies, indicating spots on the map.

"And the other?" Jacin inquires.

"Here at Mesa Two. Each within a short distance from old buried mine shafts," Sal explains, pointing to various locations.

"The question is, if the crew are all dead, who and how do they get the gold off the plane?" Paco ponders.

"According to this map, there are no roads in that area," Jacin notes.

"But a hell of a lot of abandoned mines," Paco remarks, studying the map. The storm would rule out a helicopter.

"The records show the Army finds the wreckage early the following day, no survivors and no gold. The bodies are all ashes or burned beyond recognition," Sal reveals.

"So, whoever takes the gold only has about twelve hours or less to get it out of the fuselage of the burning plane," Jacin concludes.

"Yes, in a heavy rainstorm," Sal agrees.

"Okay, Sal, I think you're on to something. Are you working today?" Jacin asks.

"No. I'm still waiting for approval of my plans from Washington. What do you need?" Sal replies.

"Raise your right hand. Do you remember what you swore the last time?" Jacin asks.

"Yes," Sal confirms.

Jacin retrieves a badge and a small leather identification wallet from his desk, handing them to Sal.

"What do you need?" Sal inquires.

"Quietly check out old newspaper articles at the Winslow library to see if there are any unusual sightings around the date of the crash. Also, see if there are any other follow-up stories about it or the gold," Jacin instructs. Chances are they never got online if the reports were from one of the small local newspapers back then.

Paco leans back in his chair, eyes fixed on the screen of his computer. Jacin stands beside him, studying a map spread across the desk.

"UFOs," Paco muses, breaking the silence.

"Or any other strange sightings in the air or the desert. Now that you're wearing the tin, read the notes I gave Karen on Doctor Torry's theories and then forget you read them," Jacin responds, his tone serious.

Before Paco can respond, there's a knock on the door, and Karen enters.

"Lieutenant, I just had a call from Kootala's grandson. Kootala took the jeep and headed into the desert. Said to call you. He has the answers you have been searching for. Meet him at Kneeling Rock," Karen announces.

Paco furrows his brows. "Where is Kneeling Rock?"

"I know where he is heading. I'm going to take the Bronco," Jacin declares, determination evident in his voice.

Paco shakes his head. "You're going chasing after some crazy old man who took his son's jeep with everything we're faced with here."

"Kootala was a friend of my father's. He is a Hopi Prophet, and right now, I could use some visions of what this is all about. I am sure Kneeling Rock is where the crash took place," Jacin explains, his gaze unwavering.

"That is the old way. No one believes in that," Paco argues.

"Then that is their loss," Jacin retorts, cutting him off.

"Do you want me to go with you?" Paco offers.

"No. Take the photographs Doc gave us and go over to Winslow Airport. Talk to Dan Haggerty. He is the head of security. See if they have a video of these guys arriving during the past month. Use the squad pickup. Karen, I'll be on my hand radio. Keep in touch. Stay on those reports."

An old man sits in a blanket in the open desert near an unusual-looking Mesa. He chants in the tongue of the ancient Hopi. Jacin parks the Bronco next to Kootala's old military jeep, walks to the man, and sits down beside him. He waits for the man to recognize he has arrived.

"Young Yazzie, have you heard of this place?" Kootala asks, his voice weathered yet strong.

"Yes," Jacin replies, his eyes fixed on Kootala's.

"Do you remember the old ways I taught you?" Kootala asks, his gaze piercing.

"Yes," Jacin affirms, recalling his teachings.

"About the ancient spirits?" Kootala prompts.

"Yes, the Katsinas," Jacin responds, his mind racing with memories.

"When I was a boy, the Katsina Eototo sent to Mother Earth a terrible storm, and the earth's movement awakened me. I stood sheltered in the hollow of a Mesa. I looked down and saw a great eagle that had fallen to earth. There was much sadness that embraced the eagle, who lay very still as the storm took away the flames. A large glowing rock appeared, and two-legged creatures came out of the rock and entered the eagle. The eagle's seven heart feathers moved with the wind, entered the rock, and I closed my eyes. I felt a black darkness, opened my eyes, and watched as the wicked black darkness spirit rose out of the depths of Mother Earth and covered the eagle and rock. What looked like the creatures was now with no body or life and carried by the wind to the heart of the eagle. A blinding light greater than the lightning that surrounded the area moved through the body of the eagle until there was only evil darkness that began to spread from the body across the desert."

"Yesterday, within the storm that moved across the desert, my eyes closed, and when I opened them, there was a dark figure of a man standing here in the desert, the Mesas off in the distance. His black shadow was not of his body but of the two-legged creatures I saw eighty years ago. As he began to turn, I realized it was your eyes I was looking through, and I woke up and came here to find the man. Within him is the black darkness. You, Yazzie, must drive him back to the fiery depth of Mother Earth. He will kill of his own, then search for others to take their bodies..." The killing will never end.

"Kootala, you have brought me the truth," Jacin acknowledges solemnly. "I will find the black darkness. Now, you must return to your son."

Jacin stands and assists Kootala to his jeep.

"I will do as you say, Yazzie. Do as I have asked," Kootala assures him before driving off.

Jacin watches the old man depart, his thoughts heavy with the weight of the task ahead. As the dust settles, he hears the click of his radio.

"Base to Unit 4," Karen's voice crackles through the radio.

Jacin picks up the radio mike. "Unit 4, go ahead, Karen."

"You have another body... Merian Air Park at Mesa point. Lieutenant Parker wants to know where to pick you up," Karen relays the urgent message.

"Leupp Triangle. I'll leave the jeep there. I will be on hand radio," Jacin responds decisively.

"Base out," Karen acknowledges, ending the communication.

Jacin arrives at the designated location and spots the county helicopter waiting in the parking lot. He walks over, and Robb opens the door for him. Jacin climbs in and puts on a headset as the chopper takes off.

"Flagstaff PD read my BOLO and called me. They have a body with the same M.O.: a head wound," Robb updates Jacin as they fly.

"That's a long way from anything. Who found the body?" Jacin inquires, his mind already piecing together the puzzle.

"A surveyor group was working in the area. Just plain luck, or we would have never found it," Robb explains.

"Is Flagstaff releasing the site to us?" Jacin questions further.

"Yes, they said they have enough problems of their own. Said they were involved in the prison break," Robb responds, providing insight into the situation.

"What about their pathologist?" Jacin probes for more information.

"Friends with Doc, they gave him jurisdiction without a bundle of paperwork. He should be at the site by now," Robb informs Jacin.

"Why these three locations? Why not just dump them in the river or down a mine shaft?" Jacin wonders aloud, contemplating the killer's motives.

"Maybe he wants us to find them," Robb suggests, his voice tinged with uncertainty.

"I don't know about that, but I think the locations may be the key to untangling this thing," Jacin muses, his mind racing with possibilities.

As they fly towards their destination, the desolate beauty of the desert Mesas stretches out beneath them.

"He's here," Robb announces, his eyes scanning the landscape below.

The morgue's helicopter comes into view, with Doc kneeling next to a body. The helicopter descends and lands on the ridge nearby.

Robb and Jacin step out of the chopper and join Doc and his assistants.

"Doc, is he the same as the others?" Robb inquires, his voice tense with anticipation.

"He is one of the men depicted in the article, but unlike the others, they did not carve him up," Doc responds, his expression grave.

Jacin takes some pictures before standing and surveying the desolate terrain.

"How in the hell does he get them to these out-of-the-way places?! There are no footprints, car tracks, or debris," Jacin wonders aloud, frustration evident in his voice.

"Did you say pictures from an article? What pictures?" What article?" Robb interjects, curiosity piqued.

Doc glances at Jacin before addressing Robb. "Show Robb the newspaper photographs. I think now he should look at what I found and what it means."

Jacin flips through the photographs on the tablet and stops at the newspaper with photographs of the passengers. Robb studies them closely before turning his attention to the latest victim.

"Oh shit! It can't be," Robb exclaims, disbelief written across his face.

"But it is. All of them were on that military plane. They were some sort of scientist," Doc confirms, his tone somber.

Robb looks around at the desert landscape, a sense of unease settling over him.

"I don't like it; not one thing about this. But I'm buying into your science fiction theory," Robb admits reluctantly.

"What are the Feds telling you?" Doc inquires, concern evident in his voice.

"Not a damn thing! They suddenly got silent and said they would get back to me, which makes me feel even more uncomfortable," Robb reveals, frustration lacing his words.

"We have been lucky so far. The papers are calling it cartel killings, and they are not that interested," Doc adds, his tone grim.

As the sun sets over the rugged desert landscape, Jacin, Robb, and Doc are left grappling with the sinister mystery that unfolds before them.

Jacin looks around for a moment.

"What kind of dark monster are you?" Jacin whispers.

***

Jacin enters the Ranger office, and Karen hands him his messages. He looks through them and gives Karen the tablet.

Jacin hands some documents to Karen. "Look these over and get copies to Rob."

Karen takes the papers. "The same assailant?" she asks.

Jacin nods. "Looks that way."

"The hole in the neck?" Karen inquires further.

"Yes, but this one didn't have knife wounds. He matched one of the scientists in the news article," Jacin explains.

Finishing his examination of the messages, he hands them to Karen. "Follow up on these two and have Makia look into this one." Karen inquires. Should I release your notes to Robb from the meeting with Doc?"

"No, not yet. He has enough to chew on after the latest killing."

As Jacin starts to walk towards his office, Karen stops him. "There's a paper bag on your desk. The man said Kootala told him to drop whatever was in the bag off."

"Did he give you his name?" Jacin asks.

"No, and I didn't recognize him, except he is from the villages of Walpi, Mesa One," Karen responds.

"Did you look in the bag?" Jacin queries.

"Whatever it is, it's in a dusty blanket," Karen answers before closing her tablet and heading towards Jacin's office.

Inside Jacin's office, Karen sees the blanket on a side chair along with an old dusty leather briefcase. Jacin is looking through a thick file of notes and drawings, holding up a metallic strip.

"What does that look like to you?" Jacin asks, handing it to Karen.

"Some kind of pin, maybe an insignia, or it could be some kind of jewelry," Karen suggests.

"Someone has tried to clean it, making these symbols easier to make out," Jacin observes.

Karen then looks at the note that came with the briefcase and reads it aloud. "This belonged to my father, Major Jon Kwahu, U.S. Army. He and his superior officer, Colonel Robert Harris, Military Intelligence Officers, investigated the crash of a USAAF Douglas C-54B Skymaster. My dear friend Kootala told me to bring this to you. It will help you to understand the Night of the Eagle."

"These files and pictures are all marked SECRET and ULTRA TOP SECRET." "This is the Army's secret investigation of the crash that these murdered men were passengers on," Jacin explains. "According to this document, the plane was not headed for San Francisco but rather White Fish Montana on the border with Canada."

"Major Kwahu was Hopi," Karen notes.

"No one is to know about these files, understand?" Jacin instructs firmly.

"Yes, Sir," Karen responds.

"No one!" Jacin emphasizes.

"What more can I do to help?" Karen asks.

"Just get today's photos and files to Robb and take care of the items in the messages," Jacin replies.

"What are you going to do with all this?" Karen inquires further.

"Find a dark hole and read all of Major Kwahu's files and maybe get a handle on what this whole thing is about," Jacin answers determinedly.

Chapter 9: Passenger 5

Paco and the head of security, Dan Haggerty, stand in the dimly lit room, their eyes fixed on the monitor displaying images of arriving passengers. The last passenger clears the frame, leaving only the static image of the empty terminal.

"That's everything in the past three weeks. You have three out of four," Dan remarks, his tone matter-of-factly.

"What about private planes?" Paco questions, his gaze intent on the screen.

Slipping in a different disk, Dan responds, "This morning, Gulfstream G700 came in about 8:30 am. A limousine met it."

A beat passes as they watch the footage.

"This is the only view we have," Dan adds, pointing to the screen.

One man exits the G7 jet, holding a collapsed wheelchair. As he reaches the bottom steps, he opens the custom wheelchair. A woman emerges, assisted by a young Asian man, and descends the steps to the waiting chair.

"Can you freeze that and move in on her?" Paco requests, his eyes darting between the screen and a photograph from Doc Torry.

"What do you think?" Dan inquires, his curiosity piqued by Paco's scrutiny.

"That's her. You able to tell me what a crash in '47 has to do with her?" Paco muses, his mind working to connect the dots.

"Not yet. Give me a print of her also and send it to Jacin," Paco instructs, determination evident in his voice.

"Let me see what else I can find out about the woman," Dan replies, picking up the phone and dialling a number with practiced ease.

"Jerry, that G7 that came in this morning. What can you tell me about the passengers?" Dan queries, his voice low and urgent.

After a brief pause, Dan scribbles down some notes on a pad.

"Thanks, Jerry," Dan acknowledges before handing the paper to Paco.

"Her name is Gloria Hines. The little guy is her personal assistant and bodyguard, Lee. The big guy is Drake Stone, her nurse. There's the tail number," Dan explains, sharing the newfound information.

"Did she mention how long she was going to be here?" Paco asks, his mind already formulating a plan.

"No, but she is staying at the La Posada Hotel on Second," Dan reveals, offering another piece to the puzzle.

"Was that a local limo rental?" Paco probes further, seeking more details.

"Yes. The driver works at the airport. We keep a file on all the drivers. Hold on," Dan replies, swiftly navigating to his computer and pulling up a file.

He prints out the information and hands it to Paco, along with a photograph of the woman.

"Here. He's a good guy. Slip him a twenty-dollar bill, and he'll give you what he knows about the lady," Dan advises, his tone friendly yet businesslike.

"Thanks for your help with this," Paco expresses his gratitude, taking the file and photograph.

"Tell Jacin he owes me a bottle of JB," Dan quips with a grin as they prepare to depart.

Paco exits the airport building, the sun casting long shadows as it begins its descent towards the horizon. He spots an attractive woman sitting on an equipment case, surrounded by several other large cases. She appears agitated. Paco approaches her with a concerned expression.

"Is there a problem, Miss?" he asks, his deep voice cutting through the air.

The woman looks up, her eyes meeting Paco's, and notices the badge on his shirt. It's clear his imposing six-foot-four frame takes her aback.

"No, well, yes. My crew missed their connection in Chicago and now won't be here until 11:30 tonight," the woman says, her frustration evident in her voice. This woman is Professor Carmen Walker, a Volcanologist.

"Where are you staying?" Paco inquires, his tone gentle yet authoritative.

"Econno Lodge," Carmen replies, her gaze dropping to the ground.

"Why don't I pack these cases in the pickup and drop you off? I'm headed that way," Paco offers, extending a helpful hand.

Carmen hesitates, unsure whether to accept his offer.

"But..." she starts, her words trailing off.

Paco interrupts her, his voice firm yet reassuring.

"But nothing. It is my job to protect and serve," he insists, a small smile playing at the corners of his lips.

Carmen looks around, realizing there's no one else nearby who can assist her. She smiles gratefully and stands up, accepting Paco's offer of help.

"Protect?" she questions, raising an eyebrow in confusion.

"From the heat, ma'am. The pickup has air conditioning," Paco clarifies, his smile widening.

Carmen's smile mirrors his as she gathers her belongings.

"Okay," she acquiesces, a sense of relief washing over her.

Paco picks up two of the cases, and she takes one, "I'll take this one, she insists."

Paco tells her to place it under his arm.

"No, I have them; these are by instruments."

They carry the luggage to the pickup, while Carmen follows suit with the smaller case. They load the luggage into the back seat of the vehicle, except the smaller case she places between her and Paco. He takes the opportunity to strike up a conversation.

"What instruments?" he asks, his curiosity piqued.

Carmen extends her hand around the case with a warm smile.

"Professor Carmen Walker. I am a volcanologist," she introduces herself.

Paco shakes her hand firmly, a look of interest crossing his features.

"Paco, Ranger. Welcome to the land of Mesas, craters, and volcanoes," he greets her warmly as they settle into the pickup.

As they drive away from the airport, Paco continues the conversation.

"You and your crew here to study our volcanoes?" he inquires, his tone filled with genuine interest.

"Testing some new equipment," Carmen replies, her eyes glinting with excitement.

"Well, they've been around here for millions of years," Paco remarks casually, his eyes flicking to the road ahead.

"I overwrote evidence of earlier geology during the Yavapai Orogeny and the Mazatzal Orogeny major mountain-building events 1.8 to 1.6 billion years ago," Carmen begins, launching into an explanation of her research.

Her voice trails off as they drive further into the desert landscape, leaving behind the sounds of an approaching passenger plane back at the airport.

***

Jacin is in the barn with Mato, his sixteen-year-old son, who has just returned home from summer camp. They're surrounded by the quiet serenity of the desert as Jacin tinkers with a CB radio transmitter. Their loyal companion, Dog, lies nearby on a small bed, dozing peacefully.

"How was camping this year?" Jacin asks, his voice tinged with fatherly concern.

"The first few days were kind of boring, but then I met Jack, and we made it interesting," Mato replies with a hint of excitement in his voice.

"That's good," Jacin responds, a small smile playing on his lips.

"Mom said you're on a big case, but I didn't see anything in the papers," Mato remarks, curiosity evident in his tone.

"We're keeping this one out of the papers," Jacin explains cryptically, his expression unreadable.

Mato shifts uncomfortably in the barn, a mix of curiosity and determination evident in his expression.

"What is it?" Jacin notices his son's restlessness and decides to indulge his curiosity.

"Why don't you tell me more about Jack," Jacin suggests, hoping to divert Mato's attention for a moment.

"You know I'm going to be sixteen in a few weeks, and I think it's time you told me more about your job," Mato responds, his tone earnest.

"You do, huh?" Jacin raises an eyebrow, slightly surprised by Mato's assertiveness.

"Yes. Maybe I want to be a Ranger someday," Mato reveals, a hint of ambition in his voice.

"I want more for you than this: a doctor, lawyer, or even your own business someday," Jacin responds, his voice tinged with paternal concern.

"Okay, then I need to know more about what really goes on outside the reservation," Mato insists, determination shining in his eyes.

"You read the papers and watch the news," Jacin points out, hoping to deflect Mato's curiosity.

"Yes, and I watch movies and video games that are all fiction about law enforcement," Mato counters, his frustration evident.

"Some of those games will give you nightmares," Jacin cautions, a note of warning in his voice.

"You just made my point. They are not real. Today, a lot of stuff isn't printable. At least that is what you're telling me," Mato argues, refusing to back down.

Jacin sighs, realizing that Mato is not easily dissuaded.

"Sixteen in a few weeks?" Jacin changes the subject, attempting to lighten the mood.

"Yes, and I don't know much about what you do that is real law enforcement," Mato presses, determined to get answers.

"Well, if I let you in on some things I get involved in, you can't tell anyone. That includes your new best friend," Jacin warns, emphasizing the importance of secrecy.

"It's not a thing she would be interested in," Mato assures him, a mischievous glint in his eyes.

"Jack is a she?" Jacin raises an eyebrow, amused by Mato's revelation.

"Yes, Jack. Her name is Jacquelyn, but she prefers Jack," Mato confirms, a small smile playing on his lips.

"So, you and Jack made things more interesting," Jacin observes, a hint of amusement in his voice.

"You're getting off the subject, Dad. Are you going to tell me about this big case or not?" Mato redirects the conversation, eager for answers.

"Okay... What do you know about cybernetics and cryonics?" Jacin finally relents, deciding to satisfy Mato's curiosity.

"Cybernetics is the science concerning the study of systems of any nature, an organism that may have both artificial and natural systems," Mato explains, demonstrating his knowledge.

"Oh! Very good. Would you consider the brain a natural system?" Jacin tests Mato's understanding further.

"It is a system that can receive, store, and process information," Mato replies confidently.

"Cryonics?" Jacin prompts, eager to gauge Mato's comprehension.

"The failed science of freezing a human body and later thawing it after they found a cure," Mato recites, his brow furrowing in thought.

"What if there was a device that, when inserted into the brain stem, accomplished cryonics' real purpose?" Jacin poses a hypothetical scenario, intrigued by Mato's reaction.

"Keeping them alive?" Mato suggests, his mind racing with possibilities.

"A way to hold a human's timeline and continue the life cycle without aging," Jacin elaborates, intrigued by Mato's insight.

"It sounds like a living artificial intelligence or a human cyborg. It's science fiction. I think I saw the movie," Mato muses, his imagination running wild.

"It's not a Hollywood movie, son, but a psychopathic killer who has been killing humans for over a hundred years. He or she may also be a living cyborg. Somehow, they have conquered the aging process," Jacin reveals, his tone serious.

"You're kidding?" Mato's eyes widen in disbelief, struggling to comprehend the gravity of Jacin's words.

"No, son and the worst part is that he or she may be from another solar system and have taken the body of an earthly human," Jacin explains, his expression grave.

"Okay Dad, hilarious. You could have just told me for whatever reason you can't tell me," Mato dismisses Jacin's revelation with a hint of skepticism.

"I told you the truth, and you cannot tell anyone, including your mother," Jacin insists, emphasizing the importance of secrecy.

Just then, Paco's voice interrupts their conversation from outside the barn.

"Anyone home?" Paco's voice rings out, drawing their attention.

"We're in the barn," Jacin calls back, exchanging a knowing glance with Mato.

Paco enters, his presence filling the space with warmth and familiarity. He spots Mato and immediately pulls him into a bear hug, eliciting a laugh from the young man.

"Welcome home, kid. Did you give the camp counselors a good time? I remember when your dad and I..." Paco begins, reminiscing about their youthful adventures.

"You want to tell me something?" Jacin interrupts, sensing Paco's urgency.

"Yes. Did you get the copies of the photographs from Dan?" Paco's expression turns serious as he gets straight to the point.

Mato glances at the CB radio that Jacin has been working on, intrigued by the mention of photographs.

"Yes, and I have Makia and one of Robb's guys at the hotel keeping an eye on her. Did you talk to the limo driver?" Jacin responds, updating Paco on the latest developments in their investigation.

"The only thing he heard was that whoever she was talking with had some solution to her condition," Paco reveals, his tone grave.

Jacin, with a sense of urgency, turns to Paco, his expression serious.

"Have you talked to Sal?" he asks, hoping for an update on their colleague's whereabouts.

"No," Paco responds, his tone distracted. "He was going to spend the night at the library." Suddenly, his expression changes, and a grin spreads across his face. "Oh yeah, I met this girl at the airport. She is something... five feet four and shaped like an hourglass, beautiful blonde hair, and a face like an angel."

Amidst Paco's description, a low voice emanates from the CB radio that Mato holds in his hands.

"KDWS is calling Bingo Bob... On U.S. 40, heading out of Winslow. KDWS for Bingo Bob, hello!" the voice crackles through the radio.

Jacin listens intently, pondering the significance of the message.

"I wonder if she knows Jack. Go home, Paco. We're going to get an early start," Jacin instructs, his mind already focused on the next steps of their investigation.

"She is a volcanologist. Do you have any idea how old the rocks are?" Paco starts to respond, but Jacin cuts him off abruptly.

"Go home, Paco!" Jacin insists, a note of urgency in his voice.

As Paco exits, Jacin turns his attention to Mato, a sense of purpose in his gaze.

"You fixed it. I want you to put this in the back of your mother's station wagon and attach the aerial to the back bumper," Jacin instructs, handing Mato the CB radio transmitter.

Mato nods, understanding the task at hand, and heads out to carry out the instructions.

"Dad, was what you said true?" Mato's voice is laced with curiosity as he turns back to Jacin.

"Yes. Remember when we had the flood, and we packed up everything?" Jacin confirms, his tone serious yet filled with a sense of familiarity.

"Yes. Where are we going?" Mato queries, his curiosity piqued.

"Your Grandma's. Bring your computer, clothes for school, and food for Dog. Mother is going to need your help," Jacin reveals, already planning their next move.

As Mato picks up the CB radio transmitter and leaves, Kele enters the scene. She moves close to Jacin, seeking comfort and reassurance.

"You heard?" Jacin asks, pulling her closer and wrapping his arm around her.

Kele nods, her expression filled with concern. "It's bad?" she inquires, her voice barely above a whisper.

"Yes," Jacin confirms, his tone heavy with the weight of the situation.

He looks down at her, their eyes meeting, and they share a brief, tender kiss, drawing strength from each other in the face of uncertainty.

.

Chapter 10: The Veterinarian # 6

The Ford Bronco, absent of any law enforcement identification, sits parked. Its occupants, Jacin and Paco, take a moment to survey the scene before them—a hotel looming in the distance. With silent agreement, they exit the vehicle, their footsteps carrying them toward their destination. A large black van is parked nearby; they enter through the side doors.

Inside the black van, Jacin and Paco find Sal and Ranger Makia. They sit at the bench on the opposite side of the doors, which provides them with a perfect vantage point of the hotel across the street. Paco, standing an imposing six feet four inches, maneuvers himself into the front passenger seat, squeezing past Makia and Sal.

"Good morning," greets Sal as they settle in.

"Did you get the emails I sent last night?" Jacin inquires, breaking the silence.

"Yes, and I spent all night at the library before coming here. I may have come up with some answers," replies Sal.

Jacin turns to Makia, "Anything new?"

"Her two guys left this morning and came back with a Mercedes van, the white one by the entrance," Makia reports.

"Okay, go home and get some sleep," Jacin instructs, concern evident in his voice.

"Okay. There's hot coffee in the back," Makia says before exiting the van.

"After twelve hours of research, I must admit, I am now a believer. UFO sightings go back over 2000 years in historical literature, paintings, hieroglyphs, and petroglyphs around the world," Sal begins, his tone filled with conviction as he hands Jacin a thick file.

"It is now an accepted fact by most of the world that UFOs exist in our skies. One of the most prevalent waves of UFO sightings happened here in 1947. The Roswell incident was just the tip of these extra-terrestrial events," Sal continues, his voice tinged with excitement.

"Did you find any articles on the DC4 crash?" Paco interjects, curiosity evident in his tone.

"Yes, but the Roswell crash overshadowed it, and eventually, it disappeared from print," Sal replies.

Jacin's cell phone buzzes, and he answers, opting for speakerphone.

"Are you in the van?" comes Robb's voice from the other end.

"Yeah. Thanks for the use of the surveillance vehicle," Jacin replies.

"Try not to break anything. It was a gift to the department from the city council," Robb cautions.

"Where are you?" Jacin inquires.

"In the hotel restaurant having breakfast," Robb responds.

"Did you see the white van?" Jacin questions further.

"Yes. If she gets in it, we take two cars and play checkers. Take primary; we will switch when needed," Robb instructs.

"Sounds good. Enjoy your breakfast," Jacin concludes before ending the call.

Sal pours coffee, offering it to Paco and Jacin, but they both decline.

"Were there any reliable witnesses to a UFO colliding with a military transport plane?" Jacin resumes the conversation.

"Not exactly. The military stated it was a pilot error brought on by harsh weather. I checked, and it was a thunderstorm heading east. Visibility was at zero," Sal explains.

"No mention of an air-to-air collision?" Jacin probes further.

"No," Sal confirms.

"What about the gold?" Paco interjects.

"No mention of it in the initial releases. However, a Washington reporter found out what they were transporting and broke the story. There were minimal follow-up stories that I could find," Sal replies.

"According to Robb's contact, the Feds investigated the missing shipment over a period but eventually dropped the investigation," Jacin adds.

"Do you mean that someone buried gold somewhere out there?" Paco questions, a glimmer of excitement in his eyes.

Ignoring Paco's comment, Jacin turns to Sal, delving into the heart of the matter.

Jacin looks at the material in the file Sal had prepared, "With what we now know and all this research, what do you believe happened?" he asks, his voice weighted with the gravity of their investigation.

Sal pauses, considering his response carefully before offering his theory.

"I think the DC4 was brought down by a UFO, either by accident or on purpose, and somehow the aliens took over the bodies of some of those passengers and took the gold," he posits, his words laden with a mix of conviction and speculation.

"And now, over seventy years later, has returned to the scene of the incident, killing each other off," Paco adds, his voice tinged with a hint of unease.

"Greed?" Sal suggests, seeking to rationalize the unfolding events.

"Maybe, but why did they return here now?" Jacin questions, his mind racing with possibilities.

"Question is, what have these aliens in scientist bodies been up to for all these years?" Paco muses, his tone reflective.

Jacin's cell phone clicks, drawing his attention to the incoming text message. He reads it aloud for the group to hear.

"She is just coming down," he announces before swiftly sending a reply to Robb.

"Did you talk to the desk?" he inquires, his fingers dancing across the screen.

Robb's response comes promptly, providing the confirmation they need.

"Yes," it reads.

"Paco, get the car," Jacin orders, his voice decisive. "Sal, wait until we're on the road, then go to the desk. Robb has planned for you to visit her room."

With a sense of urgency, Paco and Jacin exit the van. They have their mission clear.

Inside the Ford Bronco, Paco starts the car, the engine rumbling to life as Jacin settles into the passenger seat. His gaze fixates on the hotel loading area, anticipation coursing through his veins.

"Let Robb take the lead," he instructs, his voice calm yet resolute.

As they wait, their eyes trained on the scene unfolding before them, the white Mercedes comes into view. A woman in a wheelchair emerges from the hotel, accompanied by the imposing figure of Drake and the smaller stature of Lee. Swiftly, they load the wheelchair into the van, a mysterious device facilitating the process. With practiced efficiency, they close the doors and depart, disappearing into the flow of traffic.

Simultaneously, a blue sedan carrying Robb and another man emerges from the hotel parking lot, seamlessly blending into the morning hustle and bustle.

With a calculated pause, the Bronco pulls out onto the street, trailing behind the other vehicles with a careful distance.

"Hold back a bit," Jacin instructs, his eyes fixed on their quarry as they embark on the next phase of their investigation.

The large warehouse in the Winslow industrial area stands ominously as a pickup truck pulls up, pausing briefly before the roll-up door opens, allowing it entry.

Inside, a man steps out of the pickup, his purpose evident as he moves towards a lever to illuminate the warehouse's interior. Cages and animal pictures line one wall, while a large plastic curtain divides the room, concealing a mobile home nestled against the back wall. The man passes through the translucent curtain, revealing a dimly lit room divided by another plastic wall.

In the first room, a desk, chairs, filing cabinets, and various other furnishings occupy the space. Posters displaying different breeds of dogs and cats adorn the walls. In the second room, a makeshift hospital operating room is set up. The man approaches a wall adorned with video and computer monitors, activating them to surveil the warehouse's surroundings. Satisfied, he extinguishes the light and returns to the office room.

Outside, the white Mercedes van pulls up to the warehouse, halting its journey.

Meanwhile, Robb's car turns the corner and stops in another warehouse parking lot, while Jacin's car arrives at the opposite end of the street, coming to a halt next to an industrial park. A passing truck adds to the street's activity.

As the white Mercedes van enters the warehouse, Jacin receives a message through the car's radio.

"W112," Robb's voice crackles through the speaker.

"Go ahead," Jacin responds.

"I'm having the office run a check to find out who owns the warehouse," Robb explains.

"If she doesn't come out of there within an hour, call for backup, and we go in," Jacin instructs. "If she comes out, follow her, and I will stay here to see who else comes out. Someone inside opened that door."

"You don't want to take them now?" Robb queries.

"No," Jacin responds firmly. "Let it play out. She did not check out of her room, and Sal says they have not packed to leave. He is still there."

The scene shifts back to the large warehouse; the two men have unloaded Gloria Hines' wheelchair from the van. Doctor John Bigalow, a middle-aged, handsome man, meets them. Lee, one of the men, carries an aluminium briefcase.

"Gloria, you look terrible," John remarks as they greet each other.

"It's the same feeling we had when we left the ship," Gloria responds wearily. "You said you corrected this."

"This way," John directs them, leading the group towards the plastic curtain.

"Did you bring the money?" John inquires as they reach the dividing barrier.

"Did I have a choice? I have what you demanded," Gloria retorts.

John acknowledges her request, looking towards the two men and the briefcase Lee carries before opening the way to the office.

"They go where I go," Gloria asserts.

"Do they know about..." John begins, but Gloria cuts him off.

"Yes, everything! Now, can we get on with this?" she demands.

John complies, pulling back the curtain to reveal the office. Inside, he retrieves a small cooler from the refrigerator, its contents shrouded in secrecy, however we observe a small plastic box, its contents floating in a liquid substance, four index fingers. Lee sets the briefcase on the desk, opens it, and reveals stacks of hundred-dollar bills.

"Now, what is this cure?" Gloria presses, her patience wearing thin.

John opens the cooler, revealing several plastic bags containing mysterious contents nestled among dry ice.

"Each bag contains one slice of human flesh treated with a cocktail of chemicals," John explains.

"Human?" Gloria's shock is palpable.

"Yes... You will start by taking two tonight with your dinner. Warm them, but do not fry or eat them cold. They go well with rice and a little curry," John instructs.

"And after that?" Gloria probes further.

"Then one each month for the next six months, and this body will return to what it was when I transferred your 'deltaic' to this body," John responds.

"And the human you extracted these delicacies from?" Gloria questions.

"Not your problem," John dismisses her concern.

"What about the others?" Gloria presses.

"They were here, and I took care of them," John assures her, handing the cooler to Lee.

"None of this would have happened if you had not broken protocol and played tag with that military plane," Gloria scolds, her frustration evident.

"When we crashed, I made sure all of you got out alive," John begins, his voice tinged with remorse. "We had about twelve hours before that storm would let up, and they would find us unable to live in their atmosphere. You were already unconscious. The crew who were able to bring the passengers who still had a spark of life aboard our ship. For the next seven hours, I operated on each of you to insert your life 'deltaic' into these bodies."

"Then you polarized my beautiful body to dust," Gloria interjects bitterly.

"I had no choice," John defends himself. "We had to place our bodies in the passenger seats and then set the compartment on fire before blasting it with ecrona. When you woke several earth days later, we had already found the crates of gold and, using our kay-levu, shuttled them to our ship. We had just enough power to get the ship to a dead volcano and cut a path. Most of you took several earth days for your bodies to become joined with your 'deltaic,' and you could leave the ship." "Marcos assisted me in placing the deltaic' in this body, and fortunately, I recovered quickly."

"We could have returned to our world and enjoyed the rewards of our mission instead of being disgraced and abandoned on this disgusting planet in these loathsome bodies," Gloria retorts bitterly.

"My dear, it has been almost eighty years for peat sack. You're alive; be thankful for that." John retorts.

John moves behind her wheelchair, seeking solace in her presence, but she motions for Lee to stay back.

"It appears each of you have done well by your share of the gold, only to return over time to extract what you deposited individually in caves or abandoned mines in the Arizona desert," John observes.

"Yes, very well, once I learned this planet's investment strategies," Gloria acknowledges.

"This is the second time I have saved your life. I think a little appreciation would be nice," John remarks, a hint of hurt in his voice.

"You got your appreciation in that case, and whatever you're thinking will never happen," Gloria shuts down any hopes he may have harbored.

"So be it," John concedes, returning to his seat next to the case filled with money.

"When we left this desert, we agreed never to communicate unless it was vital. That is the only reason I have come back here!" Gloria asserts firmly.

"Are you going to retrieve what you have left of your share?" John inquires.

"Unlike the rest of you, I did not stick it in some hole. I took it all with me when I left on my Gatoo, then thanks to that young pilot who helped me... Well, anyway, hopefully, we will never have to return to this desert oven again," Gloria reveals her plans.

"Come with me here and let me look at your 'deltaic,'" John redirects the conversation, leading them into the operating room.

Once inside, Gloria asserts her dominance, making it clear that any misstep from John will be met with severe consequences.

"I understand," John agrees, proceeding cautiously with the examination.

"Now, I am sure you remember what this is," John reminds her, holding up a device about the size of a cell phone.

"Yes, go ahead," Gloria consents, bracing herself for the procedure.

With precision, John activates the device, allowing each to peer into Gloria's head and observe the intricate workings of her 'deltaic.' As he manipulates the device, revealing her skeletal structure and the core planted in the back of her neck at the hairline, Gloria's fate hangs in the balance, her future intertwined with the secrets hidden within her very being.

John and Gloria study the images displayed before them, assessing the condition of Gloria's 'deltaic.'

"There is no permanent damage. You will be fine," John reassures her, his voice calm and steady.

"If I am not showing improvement in a reasonable time, they both have instructions to find you and rip out your heart," Gloria warns, her tone laced with a menacing edge.

"Charming, but you will be fine. You can thank the biochemist in the body I possess for helping to discover this cure," John responds, attempting to lighten the mood.

"Are we done here?" Gloria questions, eager to conclude their business.

"Yes," John confirms, moving to touch her wheelchair. Drake, however, intervenes, removing John's hand from the wheelchair with a silent warning.

"Of course," John concedes, leading them back into the office and again handing Lee the cooler.

In the warehouse office, John issues instructions to ensure the proper handling of the flesh, emphasizing the importance of keeping it frozen until Gloria is ready to warm and consume it.

As they prepare to depart, John retrieves a file from his desk, indicating that there is one more matter to address.

"We may have a serious problem that affects us both, and your gentlemen here may be able to resolve it," he explains, handing the file to Gloria for her perusal.

Gloria examines the contents of the file, studying the photos and documents before passing it to Lee.

"Ok. Consider it a parting gift," she remarks tersely, signaling the conclusion of their meeting.

In Jacin's car, Robb's voice crackles through the radio.

"W212," he calls out urgently.

"That's it! I'm calling for backup and going in now," Robb announces, his tone betraying a sense of urgency.

"Hold on. The door is coming up," Jacin responds, his mind racing with the unfolding events.

As the large warehouse door looms ahead, the white van pulls out, followed by the pickup truck heading in the opposite direction.

"You take the van. I will follow the pickup," Jacin instructs, his voice decisive.

"I just got a message on the owner of the warehouse. A Doctor John Bigelow. He is a..." Robb begins, but Jacin interrupts.

"Veterinarian. He is Dog's vet," Jacin supplies, recalling his familiarity with the name.

"We will do this your way for now, but stay in touch. It's your ass if it goes sideways," Robb warns sternly before signing off.

"He is such an asshole," Paco remarks, his frustration evident as they continue their pursuit, the tension mounting with each passing moment.

Chapter 11: A Parting Gift

The large van sits across the street from the Posada Hotel, the evening casting a dim light upon the scene. Jacin steps into the van, finding Robb and Sal already seated inside.

"I have Makia watching his house-office. Anything new here?" Jacin queries as he settles in.

Paco enters and takes the front seat, offering a brief update. "I picked up my car and changed my clothes."

"Her two guys walked out a half hour ago, but the van was still there. We should have taken them at the warehouse," Robb laments, frustration evident in his voice.

"With what charge? We don't have anything at this point that we can prove," Jacin reminds them, trying to maintain a level head amidst the tension.

"If you're right, they have been walking around in dead bodies, killing each other," Robb counters, his concern mounting.

"Do you want to take what we have to a judge and get a warrant?!" Jacin challenges, the weight of their situation bearing down on him.

"Judge, we have these space aliens who took the bodies of six Americans over seventy-five years ago. One of them had just arrived in her private jet to meet with a local veterinarian. We think he has been killing off the other aliens." "They have also stolen thirty million in gold from the government," Paco summarizes, his words dripping with sarcasm.

"Here is something to ponder. If the crash killed them in 1947 and the vet has killed them now, is that a crime?" Sal interjects, prompting a moment of contemplation. Jacin adds, "We are still not sure the vet is one of them."

"Okay. I see your point," Robb concedes, acknowledging the complexity of their predicament.

"The other thing is if this gets out, you're going to have the FBI and every government agency, including the Army and Airforce down here," Sal warns, his voice tinged with apprehension.

"Next will come the ten million UFO groupies," Paco adds, his tone exasperating.

"I already have the captain asking me to turn in a report on these drug-related murders," Robb reveals, further complicating their situation.

"If you want to walk away, now is the time to do it. Write it up as a couple of drunks who fell off a cliff. A workman who was electrocuted and a guy who lost his way in the desert," Jacin suggests, offering an escape route from their mounting troubles.

"I didn't say I wanted out. I just want to know what we're going to do now. How do we handle these... things?" Robb presses, seeking guidance from Jacin.

"At this point, we don't know why she is here and if the vet is actually one of them or who killed the others," Jacin admits, grappling with the uncertainty of their situation.

"Did you find any answers in her room?" Paco turns to Sal, hoping for some insight.

"I think she is very sick and, as the limo driver implied, she is here to see someone to help. Other than that, nothing out of the ordinary," Sal reports, his findings offering little clarity.

"Was there a wall safe in her room?" Jacin probes further, seeking any potential leads.

"In the closet, but it was closed and sealed as usual by the hotel, so she did not use it," Sal confirms, the lack of activity adding to their frustration.

"Her guys are back, and it looks like they went shopping somewhere," Paco observes, glancing out the window.

"Did you see a cab or what they were driving?" Robb inquires, trying to gather as much information as possible.

"No," Paco responds, his gaze fixed on the scene unfolding outside.

"That's a lot of shopping," Sal remarks, his tone indicating a mixture of surprise and suspicion.

"I think we should get some sleep. Paco, you want to take the first watch?" Jacin suggests, attempting to maintain some semblance of order amidst the chaos.

"No problem. I'll call you if anything changes. I just need to get my .44 out of the Bronco," Paco agrees, preparing himself for the long night ahead.

"Robb, meet me at Doc's in the morning. All of you stay off the radio," Jacin instructs, outlining their plan of action.

"I hope the hell you have a plan by morning," Robb remarks, his frustration evident as he exits the van.

"Sal, go home and get some rest and take the next watch at six in the morning," Jacin directs, concerned for Sal's well-being.

"I didn't get any sleep last night. I am going to sleep here in my van," Sal reveals, opting to stay close to the action.

"You can crash in here," Paco offers, extending a gesture of camaraderie.

"No, you'll keep me up all night. I have a sleeping bag set up and a change of clothes in the van. See you with coffee at 6:00 am," Sal declines, preferring solitude to the company of his colleagues.

"You know we have violated at least a half dozen..." Paco begins, but Jacin cuts him off, fully aware of the ethical lines they have crossed.

"I know, but we have to let it play out; the alternative would be devastating to the entire area," Jacin admits, grappling with the moral implications of their actions.

"So, do you have a plan?" Paco presses, his voice tinged with uncertainty.

"I have a feeling the vet knows we're getting close to figuring this out. I'm counting on him to make the first move." Jacin replies.

***

The morning before dawn, the air is quiet, shrouded in darkness. Jacin's house on the Navajo Reservation stands silently, seemingly undisturbed. Suddenly, a deafening explosion erupts, tearing through the serenity of the desert.

At the Hopi Tribe Police Rangers Station, the first light of dawn casts a soft glow over the building. Karen pulls into the parking lot, her cell phone ringing as she answers.

"Good morning," Karen greets, her voice laced with anticipation.

Seconds later, the building erupts in a violent explosion, sending shockwaves through the air. Debris flies into Karen's car, shattering windows and sending her vehicle lurching forward from the force of the blast.

In Winslow, Robb exits a coffee shop, a newspaper tucked under his arm and a cup of coffee in hand. As he approaches his car, a sudden commotion catches his attention. A forklift hurtles toward him, smashing into his car with tremendous force, leaving Robb sprawled motionless on the ground.

Meanwhile, a large motorhome pulls out from a warehouse, its door closing behind it. Suddenly, a blast rips through the building, sending glass and debris flying onto the street, engulfing the area in smoke and flames.

At the Indian Health Center Hospital, an ambulance arrives, its attendants rushing to unload Robb on a gurney, his body and legs still and bloodied. Inside the hospital, Karen lies in a hospital bed, being tended to by medical staff as her worried mother waits anxiously outside.

Back at the van across the street from the Posada Hotel, Sal climbs in, his expression somber as he takes in the scene outside. Paco, already inside, observes the activity with a furrowed brow.

"Good morning," Sal greets, though his tone is far from cheerful.

"Something is going on over there," Paco remarks, his gaze fixed on the white van at the front of the hotel.

As they watch, two bellhops bring down luggage to the side door of the van, indicating that its occupants are preparing to check out.

"I just tried to call Jacin, and there was no answer. Called the office, and something is wrong with the phones," Paco informs Sal, his concern growing by the minute.

"That doesn't sound right," Sal responds, his mind racing with possibilities.

Meanwhile, at the city morgue, Jacin enters Doc's office, drying his face with a towel and carrying a rifle. Doc is at his desk, just hanging up the phone.

"The helicopter will be here in about fifteen minutes. Did you get any sleep?" Doc asks, concern etched on his face.

"Some, thanks for the use of the couch," Jacin replies, his exhaustion evident in his voice.

"Paco is looking for you," Doc informs him, sensing the urgency in the air.

"Yeah, I know. Karen is in Indian Center Hospital. They said she's going to be okay," Jacin shares, relief washing over him.

"While you were on the phone with the hospital, Robb's sister called. He had an accident," Doc reveals, his tone grave.

"Where is he?" Jacin inquires, his concern for his colleague evident.

"Indian Center," Doc responds, his expression mirroring Jacin's worry.

Jacin's cell phone rings, and he answers it swiftly.

"Where are you?" Jacin's voice is urgent as he listens to the caller on the other end.

"Have you seen them yet?" Jacin's brow furrows in concern as he processes the information.

In the large van across from the Posada Hotel, Paco speaks into his cell phone, his voice strained with worry as he converses with Jacin.

Paco's grip tightens around his phone as he relays the latest update to Sal.

"No, but her two guys just pulled up in another car. I didn't see them leave," Paco reports, his voice edged with tension.

Sal's expression darkens as he absorbs the news. His phone buzzes, and he answers. Paco continues to listen to Jacin from Doc's office. I understand; Paco has Jacin on his phone, Sal explains to the caller. "I will tell him." Sal ends the conversation and takes Paco's phone from him to talk to Jacin.

"I just spoke with my mother," Sal informs, his tone heavy with concern. "They destroyed your house last night. She is with Kele at her mother's."

In Doc's office at the city morgue, Jacin listens intently as Sal relays the information over the phone.

"I talked to them; they're fine," Jacin reassures, his voice calm despite the chaos unfolding around them. "Put me on speaker."

As Jacin continues, the gravity of the situation hangs heavy in the air.

"They also blew up the office. Karen's in the hospital along with Robb," Jacin explains, his voice tinged with worry. "The vet's warehouse is on fire, and he is on the run."

He pauses briefly before delivering the news they've all been waiting for.

"Karen is going to be okay. Not sure about Robb," Jacin adds, his voice laced with uncertainty.

With a sense of urgency, Jacin turns his words to Paco, issuing orders to ensure their next steps are executed with precision.

"Paco, call Dan. Make sure that the plane doesn't take off," Jacin commands, his voice firm. "When they leave the hotel, follow them, but do not engage. Stay in touch by phone."

In the midst of the chaos, Doc enters the room, ready to join Jacin in the unfolding events.

"Scott's here," and just heard the task force have the escaped prisoner cornered in a dead-end canyon." "It should all be over by nightfall."

Without hesitation, Jacin picks up his rifle, a sense of resolve settling over him as he heads for the door. "You coming?" Jacin asks, turning to Doc.

"Yes," Doc responds firmly. "Wouldn't miss this for the world."

Together, they exit the office, prepared to face whatever challenges lie ahead.

Chapter 12: Road Trip

Under the scorching midday heat, the motorhome bus pulls up to the pumps at a service station. John steps out, his demeanor calm and collected, as he instructs the attendant to fill up the tank.

As John enters the station, his eyes dart around, taking note of his surroundings. He casually browses the shelves, selecting a few drinks and snacks before returning to the motorhome. After paying the attendant, John requests change and a rag, feigning concern about a substance on his hand.

The attendant hands John a rag and follows him into the station. The attendant goes to the cash register with his back to John, who takes out what looks like a fat ballpoint pen from his shirt pocket.

With the rag around the pen, he moves with a swift and calculated motion. John incapacitates the unsuspecting attendant by placing the device into the back of the neck of the attendant, and he clicks the top twice. The attendant jerks and falls forward. John places the rag over the pen that is still sticking out of his neck. He takes the attendant to the garage and carefully slides him into the oil barrel. Examining the tool chest, he removes a pair of snipers' cutting pliers, pulling out the pen. He takes the attendant's hand, cuts off a finger, and pushes the man's head into the oil. He looks around, picks up the top of the barrel, and puts it in place, covering the body. Walking towards the other room, he cleans his hands and the pen device using several rags. He checks the glass counter, picks up his two hundred-dollar bills, wipes off a few spots of blood, places the finger in a rag, and walks to the door. He turns the hanging sign around to read "CLOSED."

Meanwhile, in the large van parked across from the Posada Hotel, Sal sits behind the wheel while Paco observes from the observation bench.

"You are quiet back there," Sal remarks, noticing Paco's contemplative demeanor. "What are you thinking?"

Paco's gaze remains fixed outside the window as he responds, "Worried about Karen" "and I was just thinking," "Someone may have buried a spaceship and a lot of gold somewhere out there in the desert."

Their conversation is interrupted by the arrival of Makia, whom Jacin had sent as a backup.

"They haven't brought her down yet," Sal observes, scanning the scene through binoculars. "I have a feeling they were very busy last night."

As the situation reveals, Paco instructs Makia to ride with Sal and maintain a safe distance from the target.

"If they get on the freeway, we'll checkerboard them," Paco declares before stepping out of the van, ready to execute their plan.

Meanwhile, in the helicopter above the Arizona desert, Jacin, Doc, and the pilot, Scott, strategize their next move.

"He has a motorhome bus registered to his animal clinic. I'm betting that's what we're looking for," Jacin suggests, his voice focused and determined.

Scott chimes in with his assessment of John's potential routes, outlining their options for pursuit.

"If he stays off the main highways, there are only a half dozen roads that will take him to the border," Scott explains, mapping out their course of action.

In the helicopter above the Arizona desert, Jacin, Doc, and Scott discuss their strategy as they track John's movements.

"About an 8-hour drive from Winslow industrial area and 370 miles wide choice to the Mexican border," Doc remarks, highlighting the vastness of the area they must cover.

"If I were him, I'd head to Holbrooke and take the old road to Taylor and then Pinetop," Jacin suggests, contemplating John's potential route.

"It's a gamble, but I agree," Scott concurs, adjusting their course eastward.

Doc reflects on John's meticulous planning, considering his actions in light of the mysterious sickness and the calculated elimination of his crew.

"He must have had it himself and found a cure," Doc hypothesizes, speculating on John's motivations. "He knew if they started showing up dead with those devices in their brains, it would all lead to the crash and to him." "So he removed those life-giving rods, leaving them to die."

Jacin ponders the unanswered questions surrounding John's actions, particularly his decision to spare the woman's life.

"Why didn't he kill her like the rest?" Jacin wonders aloud, his thoughts consumed by the enigma surrounding the woman's role in the unfolding events.

As Jacin glances at his cell phone, Paco's voice breaks through the silence with an update on the women's movements.

"The lady is about to leave the hotel, but I have a hunch she is not going to the airport," Paco reports, prompting Jacin to instruct him to maintain surveillance while exercising caution.

Meanwhile, in the large van parked across from the Posada Hotel, Sal and Makia monitor the white van's departure from the hotel parking lot. Sal moves out and follows the white van heading west. Towards the airport.

"They're turning on the road behind the airport," Sal observes, his intuition signalling a change in their target's plans.

As the large surveillance van rounded the corner in pursuit of the white van, chaos erupted. With a thunderous roar, Lee emerged within the open doors at the back of the white van, brandishing a menacing machine gun, sending a barrage of bullets at the surveillance van, partly shattering the bulletproof windshield and the front of the van, then another burst that further tears at the windshield and sending its occupants into a frenzy of panic. Sal keeps his head down and slows. Amid the chaos, Makia bravely returns fire, and Sal desperately maneuvers the van, trying to evade the relentless onslaught.

Despite their valiant efforts, the white van continued its relentless assault, forcing Sal to navigate the damaged vehicle through the tumultuous scene. Just as despair threatened to overwhelm them, a familiar roar echoed through the air, signalling Paco's arrival in his Mustang.

With steely determination, Paco, his arm and hand outside and braced by the side mirror he aims with his trusty Magnum .44, his resolute gaze fixed on the white van ahead. With a precise shot, he unleashed a volley that struck true, hitting Lee and several bullets to the back of the driver's seat, altering the course of the intense chase in an instant. Drake, wounded, unable to control the white van, collides with the corner curb and topples over, sliding to a stop.

Outside, Paco's Mustang screeches to a halt, the roar of its engine echoing through the desert landscape. With practiced precision, Paco ejects the spent clip and slides another one in place. Reloads his weapon, his movements swift and determined.

Meanwhile, Sal's van wheezes to a stop nearby, smoke billowing from its overheated engine.

As Paco approaches the overturned van, he spots Drake's Biretta aimed in his direction. Without hesitation, Paco's .44 is up, aims, and fires, the shot hitting its mark with deadly accuracy, leaving a gaping hole in Drake's forehead.

"Paco, check the women," Sal's voice rings out from somewhere nearby, cutting through the chaos.

Paco makes his way to the back of the van, where he finds Gloria's wheelchair overturned, her body contorted in an unnatural position. Blood stains her clothes, and her hands are still clutching a 9 mm automatic tightly, the skin stretched taut over her bones.

"Look at her hands!" Sal's voice is filled with shock and disbelief as he joins Paco at the rear of the van.

Gloria's fingers, once human, now resemble grotesque claws, the skin stretched tightly over the bones and popping through in places.

"Her face is peeling away!" Makia adds, his voice tinged with horror as he surveys the scene.

Paco grimaces, the sight before him sending shivers down his spine.

"That is just ugly. Really ugly," he mutters under his breath, his mind racing with the urgency of their situation.

Not far from the chaos, the vast expanse of the desert stretches out, silent witness to the unfolding drama. Paco turns to Makia, his expression grave.

"Not hers, yours," Your face is a mess," he says, pointing to Makia's blood-stained uniform.

Makai responds, "Glass from the windshield," turning to Sal. Call for a deputy to get him to the hospital and Doc's assistants over here. We need to clean this up before anyone else arrives.

Paco reaches into the van and removes her shawl and covers her upper body and face.

Chapter 13: A Favor For An Alien

Inside the helicopter, Jacin and Doc scan the desert floor with binoculars, searching for any sign of the motorhome bus.

"We're close to Taylor," Scott says. "I hope we called it right."

"I don't know," Doc replies. "We should have seen him by now."

Jacin pauses, then says, "I think I got him. Just beyond that ridge. He should be in view."

In the distance, through the windshield, the motorhome becomes visible.

"There he is," Scott exclaims.

"Let's hope it's not a family of eight on vacation," Doc quips.

"Move in, and let's see who is in the driver's seat," Jacin orders.

The chopper moves closer until it flies parallel to the motorhome, allowing Jacin to see the driver.

Jacin observes the driver, John, who looks back at him before reaching for something.

"Take it up quick and move above him," Jacin instructs.

As the chopper ascends, a laser beam slices through part of its right-side landing gear metal skid.

"What the hell was that?" Scott exclaims.

"It's some kind of powerful laser," Jacin replies. "Stay over him."

Jacin grabs his rifle.

"When I'm ready, I want you to move to the right and out in front just long enough for me to get a couple of shots into the engine compartment," he directs Scott.

Scott adjusts the position, maintaining a view of the cab.

"NOW!" Jacin shouts.

As Scott advances, Jacin fires three shots into the engine compartment before pulling back.

"I'm going to fire at the roof into the driver's side," Jacin announces. "As I fire the third shot, move ahead again long enough for me to get several more shots off."

Jacin targets the roof above the driver's side, then fires into the engine, radiator, and cooling blade. With a split-second opportunity, he shoots through the windshield into the dashboard before the chopper retreats.

"Take it back a little," Jacin instructs.

A blue streak slices through the motorhome's roof, clipping the helicopter's rear landing struts and damaging the rear blade cover. This makes the helicopter sway momentarily before Scott regains control, returning to a parallel position behind the motorhome.

"Now what?" Scott asks.

"Just keep your position," Jacin replies, handing his Beretta to Doc.

"Can you use this?" he asks Doc.

Doc slides back the carriage, loading it with a live bullet.

"Yes!" he exclaims.

Jacin instructs, "Lean out your side and just empty it into the front top of the bus."

The motorhome slows down, smoke billowing from its front.

Jacin readies his rifle and warns Scott, "He is going to try to take us down."

The motorhome comes to a halt, and Scott hovers to the right and back.

"Now, Doc!" Jacin commands.

Doc continues to fire into the top of the motorhome. For a few seconds, the only sound is the blades above their heads.

The motorhome's rear open ramp reveals a glowing blue vessel, similar to a wheel-less motorcycle, on which John departs from the rear of the motorhome at high speed. Jacin fires a series of shots from the helicopter. The glowing vessel speeds up and, in seconds, moves away from the motorhome about fifty yards and stops.

Down the barrel of Jacin's rifle, we see John raise his hand, holding something. Jacin fires twice, and John's hand drops as he turns and tries to ignite the vessel but falls back off it.

They watch as the riderless vessel speeds up for another fifty yards into the rocky base of a Mesa and explodes in specs of blue sparks and flames. Jacin sets the rifle down, takes the gun from Doc's hand, pops the clip out, slides another one in, and engages it.

"Move towards him slowly," Jacin commands.

The chopper moves about ten feet from John, who lies face down in the hot sand.

"Set it down," Jacin instructs Scott.

Scott brings it down to the sand but doesn't fully land. It hovers in place.

"Not sure the left skid will hold it," Scott comments.

Jacin jumps out and moves towards the body. As he moves closer, he can see one bloody hole in John's back. John's fingers are trying to reach for the small laser device. Jacin kicks it away.

John turns halfway over, revealing another bloody hole in his chest. His face is burned from the hot sand, and small pieces of flesh are just hanging loose.

"You know, ranger, I never cared for humans, but I loved the canine species, and I was a hell of a good vet," John struggles to speak. "Your pet's name was Dog, wasn't it?"

"Yes," Jacin confirms.

John's breath becomes shorter, and the flesh on his face continues to fall off.

"Stay with the special dog food 'Royal Canin's Hepatic' for his liver I recommended and no scraps," John advises.

A beat passes.

"For the dog's sake, can you do something for me?" John asks.

"What's that?" Jacin inquires.

"Don't let them put what's left of me in a jar...and step back," John requests.

"Alright... Was there a Seventh member of your crew?" Jacin questions.

"Yes. Now, step back!" John commands.

Jacin moves back as the hand under John's body moves. Without thinking, Jacin lifts the Beretta to shoot, but John's body ignites. Jacin moves back further as Doc joins him. A black darkness that surrounds the blue flame rises and then is pulled into Mother Earth. It's over!

"How the hell are we going to explain all this?" Doc wonders aloud.

Chapter 14: You Can Call Me Roy

Within the expansive tent, the steady rhythm of hammering and the whirring of an electric saw permeate the air. Jacin occupies a seat at a long table adjacent to the United States Military four-star General. Various individuals fill the space, some standing while a few take seats. The room includes Doc Torrey, Paco, Sal, Makia, Ahote, Lieutenant Robert Parker (Robb), who is now seated with crutches leaning against a chair, Karen, seated while holding crutches, the two morgue assistants, and Scott. With a swift stroke, Robb signs a document about a quarter inch thick before sliding it across the table to the General.

"Lieutenant Parker, I have spoken to your Chief inspector, and there will be no further discussion about the file that never existed," states the General.

"Yes sir, understood," Robb replies.

"I think that is everyone. Now, before you leave, let me remind you again. We have given each of you a government tax-free check. If you decide to write a book, go to the media, or mention anything to your neighbour or anyone, you can look forward to spending the rest of your life in a federal prison. Is that clear?" the General addresses the room.

Most reply with a "Yes, Sir," while others shake their heads affirmatively. The General remains seated next to Doc. He hands Doc a document. As Doc looks it over, Jacin intervenes.

"Alright, everyone, that will do it. Thank you. Sal, can you take Robb and Karen to the city in the new Ranger van?" Jacin directs.

Sal promptly gets up to assist Karen while Paco and Makia hold back as the others leave.

"Come on. I'll give you a lift back to the lab," Scott offers to the morgue assistants.

They glance at Doc, who nods. "Go ahead. I have some things to finish up here," he replies.

With that, they exit the tent. Jacin then addresses Makia and Paco, "Makia, you're on duty until six. Paco, where are you off to?"

"I have a date with a volcano," Paco responds.

Jacin chuckles, "Of course you do." " Just relieve Makia at seven."

As they depart, Makia throws a playful question at Paco, "This volcano has a sister?"

Paco grins, "Nope, just very fine instruments."

Everyone else has left except Doc and Jacin, who continue to talk to the General.

"Looks like you covered everything and more," Doc says.

"Excellent! It should all arrive first of the week," General replies.

Doc stands to leave, shakes the General's hand, and then hands him a small box just large enough to hold a fat ballpoint pen.

"Thank you, and give this to someone of authority at NASA. It may help them go beyond Mars and explore the universe," Doc instructs.

With this, Doc leaves the room.

"You have a hell of a team, Jacin, and you took a major risk of losing your job and probably worse," General remarks.

"Yes, Sir!" Jacin affirms.

Jason moves to a wooden chest against the back wall behind where the general is seated. He opens the box, takes out the leather briefcase, carries it to the table, and gives it to the General. He responds with a single question. "Did you read it all?" Jacin responds. "Yes"

"You know you could have gone public with this and what's happened here, written a book, did the media circuit, and made a fortune as the man who..." General trails off.

"That's not who I am, General. Those things would have destroyed this reservation and the City of Winslow," "What is in this briefcase? Well, hopefully, the world will never know what might have happened." Jacin asserts.

"That's true," General admits.

"These are my people, and I took an oath to protect them," Jacin states firmly.

"That I understand. Are you sure there is nothing else I can do for you?" General asks.

"No, Sir. You're building us a new home and office and have delivered some advanced law enforcement vehicles," Jacin confirms.

"I may send you a few more helpful tools of the trade," General suggests.

"You're providing my son with a scholarship to the school of his choice," Jacin adds gratefully.

"By the way," the General begins, "the young man, the boy from the bank you sent me, he entered boot camp this week. I have a feeling he is going to do well."

"I hope so," Jacin responds. "He's a good kid; he has had his share of bad luck." "Thanks to you, we have uncovered well over three billion dollars in cash and half as much in assets. You and your team solved a seventy-year-old mystery… Of course, it never happened," General says with a hint of irony.

"They tried to fit in, but greed seems to be universal," Jacin muses.

"Once again, we have found that they are here, and they are not little green buggy-eyed aliens," General concludes with a wry smile.

Jacin raises an eyebrow. "Once again?"

The General ignores the question and strides out into the yard.

As they approach, a dozen men in military desert fatigues bustle about, working on Jacin and Kele's new home and barn. Kele joins them, and Jacin wraps an arm around her.

"Mrs. Yazzie," the General greets.

"The boys call me Kele," she responds.

"Well, Kele, is it coming together the way you planned?" The General inquires.

"It's going to be perfect, General," Kele assures.

"Having met all the team today, I want to make sure you get the best appliances government money can buy," the General remarks. "I have a feeling they'll be spending more than a little time here."

He leans into Kele. "And you can call me Roy."

Kele kisses him on the cheek. "They are family, Roy."

With a smile, the General walks over to the waiting military vehicle, casting a final glance at the construction site and then at Jacin and Kele. Mato approaches, saluting the General. The General returns the salute before entering the car.

As the vehicle pulls away, we hear Mato's voice-over.

"Well, Dad, I think I enjoy being involved in your cases," Mato says. "What are we going to investigate next?"

Jacin gazes out at the Arizona landscape, lost in thought. Kele notices his distant expression.

"Come along, Mato," she says. "Let's check on your room."

"Humm...the Seventh passenger..." Jacin whispers.

****THE END****

The Hopi Rangers

Although this story, all characters, and events portrayed within these pages are purely fictional, the actual work of the Hopi Resource Enforcement Service and tribal police Rangers play a crucial role within the Hopi Tribe of Arizona. They provide an important service to the 6,946,685 tribal members who live within the twelve villages located on three mesas, which form the Hopi Reservation. The mesas are located within the Navajo Nation Reservation, which occupies part of the Coconino and Navajo counties and encompasses more than 1.5 million acres.

The Hopi Resource Enforcement Service (HRES) is extremely proud and dedicated. Its members provide effective, efficient, proactive community policing to the Hopi/Tewa villages.

HRES was created in 1989 through a Hopi Tribal Resolution. In 1994, through an additional Resolution, it was reaffirmed as a law enforcement entity to implement Tribal Ordinances and State laws.

The Hopi People

The Hopi are Native Americans who are known as one of the oldest living cultures in documented history, having migrated north to Arizona in the 12th century. The Hopi encountered Spaniards in the 16th century and are historically referred to as Pueblo people because they lived in villages. They are mannered, civilized, peaceable, polite people who adhere to the Hopi way. Their culture adheres to life in accordance with the instructions of Maasaw, the Creator or Caretaker of Earth. The Hopi belief is deeply rooted in the culture's religion, spirituality, and specific view of morality and ethics. They are guardians of the sacred land known as Hopitutskwa. The Hopi Reservation, located on high and dry land, developed a distinctive agricultural method known as "dry farming," a system of relying on water retrieval, control of wind, water, and erosion rather than irrigation. Agriculture is not only significant to their economy, but it is life-giving to them.